YOUR PERSONAL
ASTROLOGY
PLANNER

CAPRICORN
2008

YOUR PERSONAL
ASTROLOGY
PLANNER

CAPRICORN
2008

RICK LEVINE **& JEFF** JAWER

STERLING

New York / London
www.sterlingpublishing.com

STERLING and the distinctive Sterling logo are registered
trademarks of Sterling Publishing Co., Inc.

Library of Congress Cataloging-in-Publication Data Available

2 4 6 8 10 9 7 5 3 1

Published by Sterling Publishing Co., Inc.
387 Park Avenue South, New York, NY 10016
© 2007 by Sterling Publishing Co., Inc.
Text © 2007 Rick Levine and Jeff Jawer
Distributed in Canada by Sterling Publishing
c/o Canadian Manda Group, 165 Dufferin Street
Toronto, Ontario, Canada M6K 3H6
Distributed in the United Kingdom by GMC Distribution Services
Castle Place, 166 High Street, Lewes, East Sussex, England BN7 1XU
Distributed in Australia by Capricorn Link (Australia) Pty. Ltd.
P.O. Box 704, Windsor, NSW 2756, Australia

Original book design: 3+Co., New York

Manufactured in the United States of America
All rights reserved

Sterling ISBN-13: 978-1-4027-4845-5
ISBN-10: 1-4027-4845-0

For information about custom editions, special sales, premium and
corporate purchases, please contact Sterling Special Sales
Department at 800-805-5489 or specialsales@sterlingpub.com.

TABLE OF CONTENTS

Introduction	7
Moon Charts	11

CHAPTER I: ASTROLOGY, YOU & THE WORLD   15

CHAPTER 2: 2008 HOROSCOPE   31

APPENDIXES

2008 Month-at-a-Glance Astrocalendar	117
Famous Capricorns	129
Capricorn in Love	131
Author Biographies/Acknowledgments	143

INTRODUCTION

THE PURPOSE OF THIS BOOK

The more you learn about yourself, the better able you are to wisely use the energies in your life. For more than 3,000 years, astrology has been the sharpest tool in the box for describing the human condition. Used by virtually every culture on the planet, astrology continues to serve as a link between individual lives and planetary cycles. We gain valuable insights into personal issues with a birth chart, and can plot the patterns of the year ahead in meaningful ways for individuals as well as groups. You share your sun sign with eight percent of humanity. Clearly, you're not all going to have the same day, even if the basic astrological cycles are the same. Your individual circumstances, the specific factors of your entire birth chart, and your own free will help you write your unique story.

The purpose of this book is to describe the energies of the Sun, Moon, and planets for the year ahead and help you create your future, rather than being a victim of it. We aim to facilitate your journey by showing you the turns ahead in the road of life and hopefully the best ways to navigate them.

INTRODUCTION

YOU ARE THE STAR OF YOUR LIFE

It is not our goal to simply predict events. Rather, we are reporting the planetary energies—the cosmic weather in which you are living—so that you understand these conditions and know how to use them most effectively.

The power, though, isn't in the stars, but in your mind, your heart, and the choices that you make every day. Regardless of how strongly you are buffeted by the winds of change or bored by stagnation, you have many ways to view any situation. Learning about the energies of the Sun, Moon, and planets will both sharpen and widen your perspective, thereby giving you additional choices.

The language of astrology is a gift of awareness, not a rigid set of rules. It works best when blended with common sense, intuition, and self-trust. This is your life, and no one knows how to live it as well as you. Take what you need from this book and leave the rest. Although the planets set the stage for the year ahead, you're the writer, director, and star of your life and you can play the part in

INTRODUCTION

whatever way you choose. *Your Personal Astrology Planner* uses information about your sun sign to give you a better understanding of how the planetary waves will wash upon your shore. We each navigate our lives through time, and each moment has unique qualities. Astrology gives us the ability to describe the constantly changing timescape. For example, if you know the trajectory and the speed of an approaching storm, you can choose to delay a leisurely afternoon sail on the bay, thus avoiding an unpleasant situation.

By reading this book, you can improve your ability to align with the cosmic weather, the larger patterns that affect you day to day. You can become more effective by aligning with the cosmos and cocreating the year ahead with a better understanding of the energies around you.

Astrology doesn't provide quick fixes to life's complex issues. It doesn't offer neatly packed black-and-white answers in a world filled with an infinite variety of shapes and colors. It can, however, give you a much clearer picture of the invisible forces influencing your life.

INTRODUCTION

ENERGY & EVENTS

Two sailboats can face the same gale yet travel in opposite directions as a result of how the sails are positioned. Similarly, how you respond to the energy of a particular set of circumstances may be more responsible for your fate than the given situation itself. We delineate the energetic winds for your year ahead, but your attitude shapes the unfolding events, and your responses alter your destiny.

This book emphasizes the positive, not because all is good, but because astrology shows us ways to transform even the power of a storm into beneficial results. Empowerment comes from learning to see the invisible energy patterns that impact the visible landscape as you fill in the details of your story every day on this spinning planet, orbited by the Moon, lit by the Sun, and colored by the nuances of the planets.

You are a unique point in an infinite galaxy of unlimited possibilities, and the choices that you make have consequences. So use this book in a most magical way to consciously improve your life.

MOON CHARTS

MOON CHARTS

2008 NEW MOONS

Each New Moon marks the beginning of a cycle. In general, this is the best time to plant seeds for future growth. Use the days preceeding the New Moon to finish old business prior to starting what comes next. The focused mind can be quite sharp during this phase. Harness the potential of the New Moon by stating your intentions—out loud or in writing—for the weeks ahead. Hold these goals in your mind; help them grow to fruition through conscious actions as the Moon gains light during the following two weeks. In the chart below, the dates and times refer to when the Moon and Sun align in each zodiac sign (see p16), initiating a new lunar cycle.

DATE	TIME	SIGN
January 8	6:37 AM EST	Capricorn
February 6	10:43 PM EST	Aquarius **(ECLIPSE)**
March 7	12:13 PM EST	Pisces
April 5	11:54 PM EDT	Aries
May 5	8:18 AM EDT	Taurus
June 3	3:22 PM EDT	Gemini
July 2	10:19 PM EDT	Cancer
August 1	6:12 AM EDT	Leo **(ECLIPSE)**
August 30	3:58 PM EDT	Virgo
September 29	4:12 AM EDT	Libra
October 28	7:14 PM EDT	Scorpio
November 27	11:54 AM EST	Sagittarius
December 27	7:22 AM EST	Capricorn

MOON CHARTS

2008 FULL MOONS

The Full Moon reflects the light of the Sun as subjective feelings reflect the objective events of the day. Dreams seem bigger; moods feel stronger. The emotional waters run with deeper currents. This is the phase of culmination, a turning point in the energetic cycle. Now it's time to listen to the inner voices. Rather than starting new projects, the two weeks after the Full Moon are when we complete what we can and slow our outward expressions in anticipation of the next New Moon. In this chart, the dates and times refer to when the moon is opposite the sun in each zodiac sign, marking the emotional peak of each lunar cycle.

DATE	TIME	SIGN
January 22	8:35 AM EST	Leo
February 20	10:31 PM EST	Virgo **(ECLIPSE)**
March 21	2:40 PM EDT	Libra
April 20	6:25 AM EDT	Scorpio
May 19	10:11 PM EDT	Scorpio
June 18	1:30 PM EDT	Sagittarius
July 18	3:58 AM EDT	Capricorn
August 16	5:16 PM EDT	Aquarius **(ECLIPSE)**
September 15	5:13 AM EDT	Pisces
October 14	4:01 PM EDT	Aries
November 13	1:16 AM EST	Taurus
December 12	11:37 AM EST	Gemini

ASTROLOGY, YOU & THE WORLD

CAPRICORN 2008

WELCOME TO YOUR SUN SIGN

The Sun, Moon, and Earth and all the planets lie within a plane called the **ecliptic** and move through a narrow band of stars made up by 12 constellations called the **zodiac**. The Earth revolves around the Sun once a year, but from our point of view, it appears that the Sun moves through each sign of the zodiac for one month. There are 12 months and astrologically there are 12 signs. The astrological months, however, do not match our calendar, and start between the 19th and 23rd of each month. Everyone is born to an astrological month, like being born in a room with a particular perspective of the world. Knowing your sun sign provides useful information about your personality and your future, but for a more detailed astrological analysis, a full birth chart calculation based on your precise date, time, and place of birth is necessary. Get your complete birth chart online at:

http://www.tarot.com/astrology/astroprofile

ASTROLOGY, YOU & THE WORLD ♑

This book is about your zodiac sign. Your Sun is in ambitious Capricorn, an earth sign that's motivated to climb the ladder of success. The challenges you present yourself can be professional, personal, material, or metaphysical, but you give it your all in every case. Careful planning, commitment, and patience are strengths that carry you through when the going gets tough. Match the grit with some tenderness for yourself to stay happy and healthy.

THE PLANETS

We refer to the Sun and Moon as planets. Don't worry; we do know about modern astronomy. Although the Sun is really a star and the Moon is a satellite, they are called planets for astrological purposes. The astrological planets are the Sun, the Moon, Mercury, Venus, Mars, Jupiter, Saturn, Chiron, Uranus, Neptune, and Pluto.

Your sun sign is the most obvious astrological placement, for the Sun returns to the same sign every year. But at the same time, the Moon is orbiting the Earth, changing signs every two and a third days. Mercury, Venus, and Mars each move through a sign in a few weeks to a few months.

CAPRICORN 2008

Jupiter spends a whole year in a sign—and Pluto visits a sign for up to 30 years! The ever-changing positions of the planets alter the energetic terrain through which we travel. The planets are symbols; each has a particular range of meanings. For example, Venus is the goddess of love, but it really symbolizes beauty in a spectrum of experiences. Venus can represent romantic love, sensuality, the arts, or good food. It activates anything that we value, including personal possessions and even money. To our ancestors, the planets actually animated life on Earth. In this way of thinking, every beautiful flower contains the essence of Venus.

Each sign has a natural affinity to an individual planet, and as this planet moves through the sky, it sends messages of particular interest to people born under that sign. Your key or ruling planet, Saturn, is a no-nonsense, take-care-of-business influence that gives you clear feedback on real-world conditions. It helps you define limits and set goals when it's supported by other planets, but can be domineering or provoke unnecessary fears when it's not. Planets can be described by many different words, for the mythology of each is a rich tapestry. In this book we use a variety of words when talking

ASTROLOGY, YOU & THE WORLD

about each planet in order to convey the most applicable meaning. The table below describes a few keywords for each planet, including the Sun and Moon.

PLANET	SYMBOL	KEYWORDS
Sun	☉	Consciousness, Will, Vitality
Moon	☽	Subconscious, Emotions, Habits
Mercury	☿	Communication, Thoughts, Transportation
Venus	♀	Desire, Love, Money, Values
Mars	♂	Action, Physical Energy, Drive
Jupiter	♃	Expansion, Growth, Optimism
Saturn	♄	Contraction, Maturity, Responsibility
Chiron	⚷	Healing, Pain, Subversion
Uranus	♅	Awakening, Unpredictable, Inventive
Neptune	♆	Imagination, Spirituality, Confusion
Pluto	♇	Passion, Intensity, Regeneration

HOUSES

Just as planets move through the signs of the zodiac, they also move through the houses in an individual chart. The 12 houses correspond to the 12 signs, but are individualized, based upon your sign. In this book we use Solar Houses, which place your sun sign in your 1st House. Therefore, when a planet enters a new sign it also enters a new house. If you know your exact time of birth, the rising sign determines the 1st House. You can learn your rising sign by entering your birth date at:

http://www.tarot.com/astrology/astroprofile

HOUSE	SIGN	KEYWORDS
1st House	Aries	Self, Appearance, Personality
2nd House	Taurus	Possessions, Values, Self-Worth
3rd House	Gemini	Communication, Siblings, Short Trips
4th House	Cancer	Home, Family, Roots
5th House	Leo	Love, Romance, Children, Play
6th House	Virgo	Work, Health, Daily Routines
7th House	Libra	Marriage, Relationships, Business Partners
8th House	Scorpio	Intimacy, Transformation, Shared Resources
9th House	Sagittarius	Travel, Higher Education, Philosophy
10th House	Capricorn	Career, Community, Ambition
11th House	Aquarius	Groups and Friends, Associations, Social Ideals
12th House	Pisces	Imagination, Spirituality, Secret Activities

ASPECTS

As the planets move through the sky in their various cycles, they form ever-changing angles with one another. Certain angles create significant geometric shapes. So, when two planets are 90 degrees apart, they conform to a square; 60 degrees of separation conforms to a sextile, or six-pointed star. Planets create **aspects** when they're at these special angles. Aspects explain how the individual symbolism of pairs of planets combine into an energetic pattern.

ASPECT	DEGREES	KEYWORDS
Conjunction	0	Compression, Blending, Focus
Opposition	180	Tension, Awareness, Balance
Trine	120	Harmony, Free-Flowing, Ease
Square	90	Resistance, Stress, Dynamic Conflict
Quintile	72	Creativity, Metaphysical, Magic
Sextile	60	Support, Intelligent, Activating
Quincunx	150	Irritation, Annoyance, Adjustment

2008 GENERAL FORECAST:
THE INDIVIDUAL AND THE COLLECTIVE

Astrology works for individuals, groups, and even humanity as a whole. You will have your own story in 2008, but it will unfold among 6.7 billion other tales of human experience. We are each unique, yet our lives touch one another; our destinies are woven together by weather and war, by economy, science, politics, religion, and all the other threads of life on this planet. We make personal choices every day, yet there are great events beyond the control of any one individual. When the power goes out in a neighborhood, it affects everyone, yet individual astrology patterns will describe the personal response of each person.

We are living at a time when the tools of self-awareness fill bookshelves, Web sites, and broadcasts, and we benefit greatly from them. Yet despite all this wisdom, conflicts among groups cause enormous suffering. Understanding personal issues is a powerful means for increasing happiness, but knowledge of our collective issues is equally important for our well-being. This forecast of the major trends and planetary patterns for 2008 provides a

ASTROLOGY, YOU & THE WORLD

framework for understanding the potentials and challenges we face together, so that we can advance with tolerance and respect as a community and fulfill our potentials as individuals.

The astrological events used for this forecast are the transits of major planets Jupiter and Saturn, the retrograde cycles of Mercury, and the eclipses of the Sun and the Moon.

A NOTE ABOUT THE DATES IN THIS BOOK

All events are based upon the Eastern Time Zone of the United States. Because of local time differences, an event occurring just minutes after midnight in the East will actually happen the prior day in the rest of the country. Although the key dates are the exact dates of any particular alignment, some of you are so ready for certain things to happen that you can react to a transit a day or two before it is exact. And sometimes you could be so entrenched in habits or unwilling to change that you may not notice the effects right away. Allow extra time around each key date to feel the impact of any event.

JUPITER IN CAPRICORN
MATERIALIZING SUCCESS
December 18, 2007–January 5, 2009

Optimistic Jupiter is ready to climb a mountain this year. Instead of simply heading off on an adventure, the

CAPRICORN 2008

planet of expansion's passage through industrious Capricorn is a time to set goals, plan a course of action, and reach the summit of success. Jolly Jupiter is usually happy exploring the world, seeking new experiences, and expanding the mind. But Saturn-ruled Capricorn puts the giant planet in a productive mood where the name of the game is getting results. Opportunities come for those who do their homework and demonstrate the patience and commitment to prove their worthiness. There's less room for sloppiness for those who want chance to turn in their favor. Good luck is earned only by solid effort this year.

Jupiter in Capricorn is a time to turn beliefs into reality. Idealistic philosophies lose their meaning unless practice brings them down to earth. The enormous planet loves the biggest ideas, but Capricorn's practicality will test them against the weight of experience. The dark side of Jupiter's presence here is materialism that values worldly achievement more than spiritual awakening. Instead of living up to standards that may be difficult to reach, it will be tempting to lower those standards or just do away with them entirely.

Hope for a balanced approach to ambition occurs with positive trines between Jupiter and Saturn in January, September, and November. These healthy alignments between the planets of expansion and contraction bring the wisdom of self-restraint and a willingness to earn one's rewards honestly. Those who play by the rules should get what they deserve, while those who cut

ASTROLOGY, YOU & THE WORLD

corners are likely to slide right off the track and slip farther from their aspirations. The Jupiter-Saturn trine in earth signs adds conscientiousness and a capacity to put in the time necessary to attain one's goals.

Positive 60-degree sextiles between Jupiter and inventive Uranus in late March, May, and November supply a plethora of fresh ideas that help us avoid repeating old mistakes. The pragmatism of Jupiter and Saturn in earth signs has a conservative side that would normally resist untested concepts. But Uranus's aspects with Jupiter weave intuition into the year's fabric to brighten it with originality. Jupiter's friendly relationships with the planets of the old tried and true (Saturn) and new and untested (Uranus) combines the best of the past and the future.

SATURN IN VIRGO
MANAGING THE DETAILS
September 2, 2007–October 29, 2009

Saturn, the planet of boundaries and limitations, takes twenty-nine years to orbit the Sun and pass through all twelve signs of the zodiac. It demands serious responsibility, shows the work needed to overcome obstacles, and teaches us how to build new structures in our lives. Saturn thrives on patience and commitment, rewarding well-planned and persistent effort but punishing sloppiness with delay, disappointment, and failure.

CAPRICORN 2008

Saturn's passage through detail-oriented Virgo is a time to perfect skills, cut waste, and develop healthier habits. Saturn and Virgo are both pragmatic, which makes them an excellent pair for improving the quality of material life. Organizational upgrades and maintenance projects increase efficiency for individuals and organizations. Education and training become more valuable due to the increasing demand for highly specialized skills. Carelessness grows more costly, because minor errors can escalate into major problems. Systems break down easily, requiring closer attention than usual. Bodies can be more susceptible to illnesses caused by impure food or water, making this an ideal time to improve your diet. Environmental issues grow in importance as we approach a critical point in the relationship between humanity and planet Earth. Fortunately, Saturn in exacting Virgo is excellent for cleaning up unhealthy toxins produced by old technologies and in leading the way to develop new ecologically friendly systems for the future.

Saturn in Virgo highlights flaws and makes it easier to be critical of oneself and others. Yet its true purpose is to solve problems, not simply complain about them. Recognizing our weaknesses can sometimes be a source of despair, but the functional combination of Saturn's commitment and Virgo's analytical skills gives hope that effective change is well within our grasp. Small steps in a positive direction can slowly build up to a tidal wave of improvement wherever you place your attention this year.

ASTROLOGY, YOU & THE WORLD

MERCURY RETROGRADES
January 28–February 18 in Aquarius / May 26–June 19 in Gemini / September 23–October 15 in Libra

---

All true planets appear to move retrograde from time to time as a result of viewing them from the moving platform of Earth. The most significant retrograde periods are those of Mercury, the communication planet. Occurring three times a year for roughly three weeks at a time, these are periods when difficulties with details, travel, information flow, and technical matters are likely.

Although Mercury's retrograde phase has received a fair amount of bad press, it isn't necessarily a negative cycle. Because personal and commercial interactions are emphasized, you can actually accomplish more than usual, especially if you stay focused on what needs to be done rather than initiating new projects. But you may feel as if you're treading water—or worse yet, being carried backward in an undertow of unfinished business. Worry less about making progress than about the quality of your work. Pay extra attention to your communication exchanges. Avoiding misunderstandings is the ideal way to preemptively deal with unnecessary complications. Retrograde Mercury is best used to tie up loose ends as you review, redo, reconsider, and, in general, revisit the past.

This year, the three retrogrades are in intellectual air signs (Aquarius, Gemini, and Libra), which can be very useful for analysis and remedial studies that help you reevaluate what you already know so you can take your learning to the next step. Mercury has a natural affinity for the air signs, so you are empowered by your mental prowess during these times. But however intelligent you feel, don't become so enamored with the workings of your mind that you forget about the practical aspects of your body and the emotional needs of your heart.

ECLIPSES
Solar: February 6 and August 1
Lunar: February 20 and August 16

Solar and Lunar Eclipses are special New and Full Moons that indicate meaningful changes for individuals and groups. They are powerful markers of events whose influences can appear up to three months in advance and last up to six months afterward.

February 6, Solar Eclipse in Aquarius: Community Concerns
A revolutionary point of view can put an end to old fantasies and give birth to new dreams as mental Mercury and idealistic Neptune join the Sun and Moon during this eclipse. Aquarius allows a wide-spectrum view in which we can see our individual lives within the larger context of teams, groups, and community. Chiron, the Wounded Healer, also joins the eclipse point, which can increase compassion globally, give birth to new social organizations, and stir more interest in charitable activities. Charismatic leaders may emerge with fresh ideas for reinvigorating society. But it could be difficult to

ASTROLOGY, YOU & THE WORLD

determine which are capable of bringing about real change and which are simply masters of illusion.

February 20, Lunar Eclipse in Virgo: Fix What's Broken
This total eclipse of the Moon in critical Virgo reveals flaws in current systems, regardless of how much effort was put into building them. Serious Saturn conjunct the Moon reflects the hard work invested in the physical and emotional structures that are starting to fail now. A Lunar Eclipse is about letting go of the past, but both the Moon and Saturn are resistant to change. Virgo's analytical abilities permit us to justify these outmoded patterns with reason and practicality. But the Pisces Sun in opposition shows that the creative path of faith and imagination will take us farther than roads of duty, obligation, and habit. When daily details drain the joy out of life, it's clear that change is necessary. Yet we may feel the need to choose between a reality that's not fully satisfying and a dream that we fear will never come true. Fortunately, evolutionary Pluto forms a creative 120-degree trine with the eclipse that eliminates nonessential tasks to free up time and energy for more meaningful activities.

August 1, Solar Eclipse in Leo: Creativity Shines
Eclipses of the Sun are often associated with the fall of leaders. This one in the Sun's own sign of Leo is visible through central Russia and China, where changes at the top are most likely to occur. On a personal level, Solar

CAPRICORN 2008

Eclipses are reminders to tame the ego and to balance will with humility. At its best, Leo is a sign of creative expression and generosity, but at its worst it represents a petulant, demanding child. Oppositions to this Sun-Moon conjunction from Neptune and Chiron add vulnerability and engender the kind of insecurity that may provoke immature behavior. Expect drama, but don't allow it to take over. Instead of giving in to the demands of others or to your own fears, step back and permit the storm to pass. This eclipse can bring healing through self-acceptance and recognition that even the biggest stories are only chapters in the book of life.

August 16, Lunar Eclipse in Aquarius: Make New Friends
This partial Lunar Eclipse is joined with nebulous Neptune, which could bring floods and fraud into the headlines. Otherwise honorable organizations may be touched by scandal or exposed as severely underfunded. Individually, this eclipse is excellent for letting go of beliefs that don't correspond with your current reality. Outdated ideals or dreams may need to be discarded, which can be painful, but awakening to today's truth brings a breath of fresh air that clears clutter from the mind. Cooperation is the key with Aquarius, so recognizing where friends and allies are more hindrance than help is important.

Remember that all of these astrological events are part of the general cosmic weather for the year, but will affect us each differently based upon our individual astrological signs.

2008 HOROSCOPE

CAPRICORN

DECEMBER 22–JANUARY 19

CAPRICORN

OVERVIEW OF THE YEAR

Optimistic Jupiter is in ambitious Capricorn this year, making it a great time for major expansion and significant personal growth. Traditional astrology's most fortunate planet brings opportunities for increased public recognition, as well as a deeper understanding of yourself. This enables you to recognize your past patterns and see how your successes and failures are connected in meaningful ways. Your ambitions are empowered by these insights, allowing you to plan with foresight and common sense. It's vital, though, to trust yourself, rather than letting the opinions of others weigh too heavily now. Jupiter in your 1st House of Self represents the power of your innate wisdom. Even if you miscalculate and make a mistake, you can quickly learn from it and adjust your course of action accordingly. **There is no time to settle for less in your life, either personally or professionally.** Standing still is the least desirable option. Aim high and boldly step forward to raise your life to the next level.

CAPRICORN 2008

Saturn, the planet of hard, cold reality—and the ruler of your sign—is outward bound this year, too, as it occupies your 9th House of Travel and Higher Education. Work-related trips are not as much fun as a week spent on the beach, but can certainly elevate your professional profile. Taking classes or doing independent study is a definite asset for advancing your career. Serious Saturn and optimistic Jupiter form harmonious trines with each other on January 21, September 8, and November 21 that align your current reality with your future hopes. This combination helps you organize plans with a healthy balance of the real and the ideal to ensure your success. On November 4, dutiful Saturn makes the first of five challenging oppositions with independent Uranus that recur through 2009 and 2010. **If the weight of responsibility or drudgery of routine is too great, you may need to force a break to find some breathing room and reassess your situation.** The long-term purpose of this aspect is to reconstruct your life in a way that allows you more freedom of expression and establishes a healthy balance between security and surprise.

OVERVIEW OF THE YEAR

Slow-moving Pluto's fifteen-year transit of your sign continues a powerful process of transformation that saw a boost when Jupiter joined this deep, dark planet on December 11, 2007. Visions of major change that were stirred by fear or desire will rumble below the surface throughout this year and can shake your normally stoic view of reality. **You sense that there is so much more to be gained from life; Pluto's message is that letting go is a prerequisite for satisfaction**. Outmoded beliefs about yourself may confront you dramatically to show you how they still shape your thinking. These are golden opportunities to recognize where change is imperative. Many chances to purge old habits will occur this year, but they will be especially potent when mental Mercury, the willful Sun, and active Mars engage Pluto on December 12, 22, and 28.

CAPRICORN 2008

PURSUIT OF HAPPINESS

The personal growth spurred by expansive Jupiter's passage through your sign is bound to alter your relationships this year. Caring Cancer in your 7th House of Partnerships tends to make you particularly protective of your spouse. Nurturing others can be such a priority that you unconsciously conceal your needs. However, the magnifying power of Jupiter in your 1st House is reflected through its opposite, the 7th House. Just as you expect more for yourself now, your need for romantic and emotional fulfillment is increasing too. Pressure on a current relationship will force it to grow or, perhaps, begin to unravel. If you bury your feelings, the long-term costs of distrust and disappointment may be greater than whatever price you pay right now. A Solar Eclipse in dramatic Leo on August 1 occurs in your 8th House of Intimacy, where it initiates changes in how you connect on the deepest levels. Open your heart to take more risks by expressing your desires—the first step toward a more satisfying relationship.

OVERVIEW OF THE YEAR

LADDER OF SUCCESS

Professional advancement is quite likely this year if you put in the effort to elevate your profile. It's possible that your ambitions can no longer be contained in someone else's employ, leading you to start your own business. The strategic Jupiter-Saturn trines on January 21, September 8, and November 21 are excellent for charting your career course, whether you're self-employed or seeking a promotion within an organization. Mercury, the communication planet, is retrograde in your 6th House of Work from May 26 until June 19 and your 10th House of Career from September 24 through October 15. Avoid making major moves during these periods, which are better suited for research and review than initiating new projects.

CAPRICORN 2008

UNEXPECTED SOURCES

You tend to take a very practical and down-to-earth approach to earning money, but this year more cash can come your way if you're experimental. Uranus, the ruler of your 2nd House of Income, picks up favorable sextiles from generous Jupiter on March 28, May 21, and November 12. These supportive aspects could improve your finances in unexpected ways. A sudden windfall or bright new idea might put you on the road to increased prosperity. Thinking outside the box increases your odds of discovering one of these veins of material success, so an open mind could be your greatest resource this year.

OVERVIEW OF THE YEAR

WATCH YOUR APPETITE

Expansive Jupiter in your 1st House of Physicality makes this an especially important year to take care of your body. This indulgent planet allows you to put on extra pounds more quickly than usual; fortunately, you are more motivated to exercise as well. This combination could lead to excesses in both directions with swings in diet, appetite, and behavior that might feel fine now but could produce problems in the future. Establish goals and guidelines for consumption and activity, but be flexible enough to allow exceptions from time to time. Jupiter's judgmental side is not an asset to good health, which is better served by forgiveness than guilt.

CAPRICORN 2008

THINK BEFORE YOU ACT

You may be so occupied with your own activities and ambitions this year that home and family get less attention than usual. However, the Sun's entry in your 4th House of Foundations on March 19 could spark a desire to enhance your living space—or might reveal a budding domestic crisis that requires action. Avoid a tendency to seek a quick fix that instantly resolves the problem; haste will only add fuel to the fire. A slower approach will take more time but also produce a happier outcome. Impatient Mars—the ruler of your 4th House—conjuncts Saturn on July 10, focusing your energy onto family obligations. Think carefully about what commitments you're willing to assume before agreeing to any significant changes in your relationships or daily routine.

OVERVIEW OF THE YEAR

♑

TRAVEL FOR A PURPOSE

Saturn, your ruling planet, is transiting your 9th House of Higher Thought and Faraway Places this year, putting you in a serious state of mind. Examining the meaning of your life is not an abstract exercise but rather a helpful step in building a bridge between where you are and where you want to go. Studying philosophy, religion, metaphysics, or foreign cultures enriches you with a wider perspective to support your goals. Don't take travel lightly, however—it could be more arduous than usual right now. Instead of visiting ten cities in two weeks, for example, concentrate on deepening your experience of one or two places. Journeys may be more complicated around February 20 when a Lunar Eclipse falls in your 9th House, and in mid-August when restrictive Saturn joins sociable Venus and mobile Mercury.

CAPRICORN 2008

TRUST YOUR INTUITION

The worlds of spirituality, dreams, and imagination become more tangible for you this year. Jupiter, the ruler of your 12th House of Soul Consciousness, in your physical 1st House puts you in direct contact with these sources of inspiration. You may feel guided in your actions, as if you are being carried forward by forces greater than your own. Have faith in what you're doing, even if you can't come up with a rational explanation for every move. This is a time to trust the universe by learning how to ride its energy waves, rather than having to paddle so hard to get where you want to go.

RICK & JEFF'S TIP FOR THE YEAR
The Power of Positive Thought

In the ongoing struggle between your hope for more and the fear of losing what you already have, go for hope this year. Overcoming a tendency to wrap your ambitions in a blanket of doubt called "reality" is relatively easy now. Whenever you encounter an obstacle, step back from it instead of attacking the problem or simply giving up. Lucky Jupiter is on your side and will provide you with solutions when you take the time to let them develop slowly. This isn't about being passive; just allow your natural wisdom to evolve and give you the answers you need.

JANUARY

JANUARY

♑

CONTROLLED CHAOS

You have a natural ability to turn new ideas into reality, and it's bolstered by the New Moon in methodical Capricorn on **January 8**. The annual conjunction of the creative Sun and nurturing Moon in your sign receives a supportive sextile from inventive Uranus, blending originality with discipline—a perfect combination for putting more spice into your life. Expansive Jupiter may send you on a detour into fantasyland with an impractical semisquare to dreamy Neptune on **January 12**. However, the bubbles of illusion settle back down to earth on **January 21** when Jupiter aligns in a constructive trine with your realistic ruling planet, Saturn. This positive aspect first appeared last spring and will return on **September 8 and November 21** to give you the kind of strategic perspective on your future that's essential for long-range planning.

The Full Moon in generous Leo on **January 22** lands in your 8th House of Deep Sharing to shed light on intimacy and trust issues, altering the nature of your closest relationships. Honesty and high hopes are your allies as you learn that giving

CAPRICORN 2008

more gets you more in return. Potent Pluto enters your sign on **January 25**, where it will stir the roots of your soul; it then retreats to Sagittarius on **June 13** before returning to Capricorn on **November 26**, where it will stay for fifteen years. The immediate effect may not be obvious, but a powerful and long-lasting transformation trend is under way. Informative Mercury begins a three-week retrograde cycle in your 2nd House of Income on **January 28** that is better for reorganizing finances and repairing resources than spending freely. On the other hand, energetic Mars goes direct on **January 30** to jump-start stalled work projects or motivate you to improve your health.

KEEP IN MIND THIS MONTH

Strong emotional exchanges can leave you feeling unsafe, but if you avoid hasty reactions you'll discover a solid place to stand.

JANUARY ♑

KEY DATES

★ **JANUARY 6**
tough love
A slick sextile between the Sun and Uranus sparks creativity and an eagerness for new experiences. However, a tense square between demanding Saturn and sensitive Venus can limit the love or approval you feel from others and possibly make you doubt yourself. Acting independently is a quick and easy solution, but doing the hard work of digging in and dealing with relationship issues will have more meaningful and lasting effects.

★ **JANUARY 13-14**
incomplete message
Mental Mercury and the Sun both tangle with restrained Saturn on **January 13**, which can make it more difficult to get your message across. If you are frustrated by someone's lack of understanding, don't push the point. Unless detailed information is vital, settle for communication that conveys the general idea. A brilliant and sharp-edged quintile between active

Mars and productive Saturn on **January 14** helps you come up with inventive solutions and clever shortcuts to accomplish difficult tasks without breaking a sweat.

★ **JANUARY 20–21**
unorthodox approach
The Sun enters innovative Aquarius and your 2nd House of Resources on **January 20**, awakening new ideas about making money and maximizing your talents. Socially conscious Aquarius reminds you that being of service to others can also be financially rewarding. The Sun's unsteady semisquare with Uranus, Aquarius's ruling planet, on **January 21** brings out your rebellious side. Turning that unconventional attitude in a creative direction gives you a sense of freedom and a fresh appreciation for your abilities. The harmonious trine between optimistic Jupiter and practical Saturn on the same day provides a well-organized framework for your ambitions, leading you to future success.

JANUARY   ♑

SUPER NOVA DAYS

★ **JANUARY 24–25**
change of heart
Sweet Venus conjuncts dark Pluto on the morning of **January 24**, pushing relationship issues to the edge and arousing intense feelings of desire or distaste. Letting go of the past now opens the way for deeper love later. Venus then enters the safe realm of Capricorn, turning fear and desire into action and resolve. Pluto's entry into Capricorn on **January 25** begins a transformative process that can ultimately increase your power and sense of purpose.

★ **JANUARY 29–30**
safe landing
A slippery Venus-Neptune semisquare early on **January 29** serves up romantic fantasies and uncertainty about your self-worth. That night, however, Saturn forms a strengthening trine with Venus to stabalize emotions and relationships. Active Mars awakens from its retrograde state on **January 30** in your 6th House of Routine, sending a "go" signal for making changes at work.

FEBRUARY

FEBRUARY

FINANCIAL FANTASY

Two eclipses are the key astrological events this month. An intelligent Aquarius Solar Eclipse on **February 6** lands in your 2nd House of Money. This special New Moon should stimulate fresh income-producing ideas; however, disorienting Neptune's conjunction to the eclipse may blur your usual good sense and tempt you to spend carelessly. Investing in objects and activities that inspire you will be positive as long as your dreams are balanced with a strong dose of realism. Maintaining a down-to-earth attitude will be easy during the practical Virgo Lunar Eclipse on **February 20**, but it falls in your 9th House of Faraway Places, where it can create travel problems. The 9th House is also associated with philosophy, religion, and higher education, so this eclipse may push you to consider your need for further schooling or to question your beliefs. Serious Saturn is conjunct the eclipse, defining real issues that stop you from hitting the road or presenting obstacles while you're out of town. Fortunately, powerful Pluto harmoniously trines Saturn and the Moon, focusing your intentions

CAPRICORN 2008

and helping you transform a frustrating experience into a deeply fulfilling one.

Attractive Venus enters Aquarius and your resourceful 2nd House on **February 17**, a time to put more pleasure in your experience bank. Creating joy in your life has long-term benefits to your material and emotional well-being. Fun is not a distraction from the serious business of survival; it's vital to your future success. Mercury, the communicator, turns direct on **February 18**, and its forward shift enables a freer flow of information. Data that was lost and details that were overlooked are likely to come back into present focus.

KEEP IN MIND THIS MONTH

Finding the connection between inspiration and making it real takes time. Don't rush the process.

FEBRUARY ♑

KEY DATES

★ FEBRUARY 1
sweet rewards

Astrology's two most fortunate planets, Venus and Jupiter, join up in your sign to reward you with well-earned delight. Your social and organizational skills mesh perfectly, making you an ideal leader, a trusted friend, and a desirable partner. A refined taste and a strong appreciation of what makes people and things valuable helps you get the best of both. You gain trust, affection, and approval because you've proven your worth over a long period of time.

★ FEBRUARY 6–7
play without punishment

A smooth sextile between well-behaved Venus in Capricorn and inventive Uranus on **February 6** makes it safe to experiment with your style and social life. A new look or unconventional form of fun may be silly, but no one is going to think any less of you for trying. Fortunately, you are able to enjoy this sense of freedom without having to pay a price for it. A talented

CAPRICORN 2008

quintile between active Mars and responsible Saturn on **February 7** suggests original ways to resolve tough problems at work with surprising ease.

★ FEBRUARY 13-14
romantic realignment
An uncomfortable quincunx between Venus and Mars on **February 13** corresponds with a clash of styles that can put stress on your relationships. Try to understand if others don't live up to their commitments; applying pressure may only push them away. A more harmonious mood prevails on Valentine's Day, **February 14**, with a dynamic Sun-Mars trine, energizing you and opening your mind wide enough to overcome yesterday's differences.

SUPER NOVA DAYS

★ FEBRUARY 20-21
delayed gratification
The Virgo Lunar Eclipse on **February 20** is a Sun-Moon opposition in the mental 3rd and 9th Houses of your chart. Stubborn Saturn's conjunction with the Full Moon may unnerve

FEBRUARY

you with doubt or confront you with a critical adversary. Don't fake it if you don't have the facts to fight as an equal. If you lack the information you need to make your case, further education on the subject may be in order. Sensual Venus is sidetracked by duties when it quincunxes Saturn on **February 21**. The most delightful plans can fall by the wayside as responsibility comes calling. Reschedule, if necessary, rather than completely sacrificing the good time you were expecting.

★ **FEBRUARY 24**
limited resources
A sober Saturn-Sun opposition can put you on the defensive or burden you with obligations that may not be yours to manage. Demonstrating your commitment to help others is one thing; agreeing to provide unlimited service is another. Respecting your own time and energy will allow you to make only those promises that you can keep without wearing yourself out.

MARCH

MARCH

CONTROLLED INTENSITY

The New and Full Moons this month are power-packed transformational events that can alter your thinking and shift your responsibilities. The psychic Pisces New Moon on **March 7** shocks your mind with strange ideas and surprises due to its close conjunction with electrifying Uranus in your 3rd House of Communication. Your daily routine may be shaken, but what you can gain from a flash of intuition is more valuable than a temporary loss of control. The Full Moon in gracious Libra on **March 21** is closely square potent Pluto and impatient Mars, a combination that can provoke you to take extreme action at home or at work. Pressures on the job or within your family can push your emotional buttons, and you're likely to react strongly. You may be tempted to strike back—but remember that this can be destructive if you're not crystal clear about your intentions. You have the ability to eliminate major obstacles now, opening the way to greater satisfaction and a more effective use of your unique talents if you apply these intense feelings in a creative and conscious manner.

CAPRICORN 2008

Extravagant Jupiter in cautious Capricorn forms a tense sesquisquare with Saturn on **March 18**—repeating on **June 26 and January 30, 2009**—that could threaten or slow down a major project. A closer look at details, however, will reveal a more efficient way to advance your interests. The Sun's entry into front-runner Aries on **March 20** marks the Spring Solstice and the beginning of the astrological year. The Aries Sun's spontaneous energy is severely tested by squares from Mars and Pluto that can turn playtime deadly serious. Jupiter brilliantly sextiles Uranus on **March 28**, bringing sudden inspiration now and repeating on **May 21 and November 13**.

KEEP IN MIND THIS MONTH

Focus on one task at a time. A major breakthrough is possible now, but only if you apply your total attention.

MARCH   ♑

KEY DATES

★ MARCH 4
make your move
Passionate Mars slips into your 7th House of Partnerships to bring a new level of dynamism to your relationships. This is an excellent time for you to take the initiative with others, deepening your current connection or beginning a new one. This transit is also beneficial for going public with a plan or project. You might encounter more aggressive individuals who try to force their agendas on you. Compromise is a much better response than combat.

SUPER NOVA DAYS

★ MARCH 7-8
when push comes to shove
The explosive New Moon conjunct Uranus on **March 7** occurs in the midst of an exact opposition between Mars and Pluto, a potent pair that tends to push issues to the edge. There's no easy retreat now: You may have little choice but to make a major change or just give up on the relationship. The Sun's union with

unpredictable Uranus on **March 8** while the Moon is in impulsive Aries is a volatile combination that could make you lose your cool. Yet this can be productive if it forces you to address a problem you've been previously unwilling to face.

★ **MARCH 14–15**
just out of reach
A sturdy Mars-Saturn sextile on **March 14** helps you work efficiently, even with irrational partners. Mental Mercury's entry into sensitive Pisces feeds your imagination, but also demands a gentler tone in your communication. A tough opposition between demanding Saturn and sweet Venus on **March 15** makes every reward hard-earned. If you feel underappreciated, remember that recognizing the source of your dissatisfaction can be a strong first step toward rectifying it.

★ **MARCH 21–23**
no regrets
The accommodating Libra Full Moon on **March 21** lands in your 10th House of Career

MARCH

and Public Responsibility, which normally implies a need to negotiate and compromise. Yet an "all or nothing" Sun-Pluto square makes it hard to find a common point of agreement. You may have to burn a bridge now—just make sure that you're willing to pay the price before striking a match. A Sun-Saturn quincunx on **March 23** continues the theme of potential conflict with authority figures. This time, though, you have more room to maneuver and can make smart adjustments to save the situation from turning ugly.

★ **MARCH 27–28**
taste test
Fast thinking prevails as intellectual Mercury joins inventive Uranus and sextiles philosophical Jupiter on **March 27**. Delicious Venus also aspects these stimulating planets on **March 28** when they form their exact sextile, attracting you to eccentric people and unorthodox pleasures. Breaking your own rules about spending or loving is worth the risk right now if it expands your palette of delight.

APRIL

APRIL

DOWNSHIFTING

You start the month at full speed, but will likely mellow out before it ends. The fiery Aries New Moon on **April 5** in your 4th House of Roots is supercharged by tense squares from impatient Mars and excessive Jupiter—lifting your ambition to.a higher level. While this may be the catalyst you need to advance your career, transform your home, or even relocate, it's very possible that you may take on too much, too soon. It's not your habit to allow impulsiveness to lead you astray, and slowing down a bit will help you maintain control of these turbulent times. Mental Mercury and romantic Venus entering speedy Aries on **April 2 and April 6**, respectively, excite your head and heart. This can be thrilling, but you may rush past important details that skew your normally sound judgment.

The pace starts to slow on **April 17** when Mercury enters patient Taurus in your 5th House of Romance, Children, and Creativity, followed by the Sun on **April 19**. Take the time to savor life's pleasures during this playful and sensual period. The Full Moon in passionate Scorpio on **April 20**

CAPRICORN 2008

can increase emotional intensity, especially with friends and groups. Yet serious Saturn and powerful Pluto form stabilizing trines to the Full Moon to turn these deep feelings in a productive direction. Additionally, garnering support from others for a personal project will accelerate its development. Sweet Venus enters easygoing Taurus on **April 30** to increase your potential for pleasure. Its four-week stay in the most playful part of your chart rewards you with delicious experiences as a lover, parent, or performer when you stop working and allow yourself to enjoy these well-deserved treats.

KEEP IN MIND THIS MONTH

Push hard when the opportunities to advance your interests arrive, but avoid forcing issues that are not yet ripe for action.

APRIL

KEY DATES

★ APRIL 6
timely intervention

This may be a less-than-lazy Sunday, with Venus's entry into rowdy Aries followed by its tense square to unyielding Pluto. You may see unresolved relationship issues rise to the surface, which is better than burying them in resentment. Even if hurt feelings and disappointment seem too hard to face, a mature Sun-Saturn sesquisquare requires you to be an adult. Addressing uncomfortable concerns now earns you respect and keeps a situation from becoming even messier.

★ APRIL 10-11
managed growth

An expansive Sun-Jupiter square on **April 10** encourages you to promise too much or express your opinions too bluntly. Another tense square, this one between chatty Mercury and feisty Mars, intensifies the day with anger, irritability, or impatience. A small disagreement could blow up into a major battle, so it's wise to temper your intemperate comments. Strong convictions and grand ambitions are allies for growth, but a demanding Mercury-Saturn sesquisquare on **April 11** reveals any flaws in your plan—a reminder to stick closely to the facts.

★ **APRIL 14**
don't take it personally
Active Mars is mashed by an unyielding semisquare from strict Saturn that permits no deviation from the rules. If your efforts are thwarted by another person, providing clear and calm direction will go over better than making demands. Pride can impede progress if either one of you puts personal issues before the task at hand. Progress may be slow, but concentrated effort can finish off a difficult job.

★ **APRIL 18-19**
hurry up and wait
Mercury forms a grand trine with Saturn and Pluto on **April 18**, making you a more powerful communicator. Your ability to add urgency and clarity to any conversation commands attention. But the joy of the Sun in Taurus entering your

APRIL

5th House of Fun and Games on **April 19** may be delayed by a less-than-generous sesquisquare between tough Saturn and soft Venus. Your hard work might not be matched by the recognition you receive, so put in the effort to satisfy yourself now. Hopefully others will come to appreciate it later.

SUPER NOVA DAYS

★ **APRIL 21-24**
shake, rattle, and roll
A stable Sun-Saturn trine on **April 21** builds self-trust and puts you on a solid foundation to handle the upcoming high-powered aspects. Dynamic Mars trines revolutionary Uranus on **April 22,** a sure sign of inventiveness and originality, breaking you free from limiting patterns in partnership. Emotions run high, though, on **April 24**: Venus in stubborn Taurus is stressed by a square from pushy Mars and an opposition to ravenous Jupiter. You may feel blindsided by increased demands in relationships, excessive expenses, or extreme anger. Ride the wave of passion by taking healthy risks instead of futilely trying to hold back the tide.

MAY

MAY

MANIFEST YOUR DREAMS

Four planets change directions this month. The action starts with pragmatic Saturn's forward turn on **May 2**, enabling you to transform blue-sky ideas into down-to-earth reality. This direct shift of your ruling planet may reveal practical limitations that can dampen your dreams, but this is only to reshape them into a workable form. Expansive Jupiter, on the other hand, begins its retrograde cycle on **May 9**, reminding you to consolidate gains, restrain growth, and manage your physical resources more carefully. Idealistic Neptune and rational Mercury both go retrograde on **May 26**. Neptune's reverse turn, a subtle influence that will last for months, brings inspiration from within, signaling a growing faith in yourself and your untapped potential. Mercury retrograde in your 6th House of Work and Service requires greater attention to detail on the job, where petty errors and miscommunication could cause problems. A change of mind about your tasks and duties is possible during the next three weeks, so avoid locking yourself into any long-term commitments at this time.

CAPRICORN 2008

The New Moon in indulgent Taurus on **May 5** plants seeds of romance and creativity in your playful 5th House. You can feel young and innocent, opening yourself to simple pleasures and sensual delight. Generous Jupiter's supportive trine to this Sun-Moon conjunction shows you ways to make these feelings last, transforming them into enduring sources of joy that remind you to have fun in your overly serious moments. The intense Scorpio Full Moon on **May 19** in your 11th House of Groups squares nebulous Neptune, which can wear you out when you're part of a team. While altruistic activities with others are rewarding, limit your responsibilities to keep them from becoming a burden.

KEEP IN MIND THIS MONTH

Small but solid steps will take you far, while giant leaps forward are more likely to leave you out on a limb.

MAY ♑

KEY DATES

★ **MAY 1–3**
down to business
Loving Venus forms supportive trines with tough guys Saturn and Pluto on **May 1** that help you cut to the chase in relationships. You can dig deeply to find value while also reducing waste in your financial and personal life. Saturn goes direct on **May 2**, adding a serious tone to the day as chatty Mercury enters clever Gemini. The communication planet is usually curious and flexible in the sign of the Twins, but its challenging quincunx with Pluto and square to Saturn on **May 3** intensify conversations with control issues and can darken your thoughts with doubt.

★ **MAY 9–12**
creative enterprise
Macho Mars storms into dramatic Leo on **May 9**, setting off sparks of passion in your 8th House of Deep Sharing. Your emotions are stirred by powerful people—some who attract you strongly and others you want to avoid.

CAPRICORN 2008

It's not easy aligning yourself with innovative partners, but it might be worth the effort. The Sun trines Jupiter and sextiles Uranus on **May 12**, bringing enormous powers to life with bright ideas and bold action.

★ **MAY 18**
boundless joy
Vivacious Venus creates a delightful trine to Jupiter as well as a sextile to Uranus, and both open you up to unconventional forms of fun. A feeling of confidence and generosity allows you to shine in any group. This is a great time to express your feelings openly and share the joy that's in your heart with your family, a lover, or friends old and new.

SUPER NOVA DAYS

★ **MAY 20–22**
the call of duty
The Sun's entry into jumpy Gemini on **May 20** could make you nervous about having too much to do. But a clever Mercury-Saturn quintile the same day and a purging Sun-Pluto quincunx the next show you how to cut through

MAY

clutter and set priorities. The Jupiter-Uranus sextile on **May 21** is another source of inventiveness that can get you out of a sticky situation. Yet complex conditions on **May 22** pull you in two directions. You have a naturally strong sense of duty—but there's a part of you that yearns for freedom now as well. Following the rules can be too restricting, so you may need to create new ones to meet your obligations in a more interesting way.

★ **MAY 26**
self-assessment
The information planet, Mercury, turns retrograde in your 6th House of Work, while a stressful Venus-Saturn square can leave you feeling unappreciated. The upside of this tense aspect, though, is a clear recognition of your worth, which could even lead to a change of employment. Whether you're ready for such a drastic move or not, greater awareness of your assets will eventually lead to greater rewards.

JUNE

JUNE ♑

INNER TRANSFORMATION

This month's New and Full Moons illuminate the service sectors of your chart, but there's also plenty of social activity on the way—two planets are now entering your 7th House of Partnerships. The jaunty Gemini New Moon on **June 3** is joined by artistic Venus and cerebral Mercury, and supported by a smart sextile from energetic Mars that sparks bright ideas in 6th House of Work and Hobbies. The plethora of possibilities may overwhelm your usual good sense of order and time management. Try to limit your distractions, especially now that Mercury retrograde challenges your ability to handle details. Pluto backs out of Capricorn on **June 13** for one last visit to philosophical Sagittarius, and your 12th House of Secrets, until **November 26**. This gives you more time to look within and complete unfinished business before the intense work to come later this year. The extravagant Sagittarius Full Moon on **June 18** conjuncts transformative Pluto and squares rebellious Uranus, a surefire sign of explosive moods, unexpected crises, and radical shifts of perspective. Since it's in your private 12th

House, all this action may be so internal that others don't even notice your turmoil. The profound changes may have more to do with your spirituality and connection to nonmaterial worlds than with the external one.

More visible activity occurs in relationships, both personal and professional, when Venus enters your 7th House on **June 18**, followed by the Sun on **June 20**. These are favorable times to reach out to others: You're likely to find sympathetic support and warm companionship more easily than you might expect. Communicative Mercury turns direct on **June 19**, underscoring how critical it is to extend yourself to enrich a current relationship or initiate a new one.

KEEP IN MIND THIS MONTH

Exploring unfamiliar ideas and emotions can be enlightening—and it's completely safe if you just observe and don't take action on all of them.

JUNE

KEY DATES

★ **JUNE 6-9**
time for play
An intense Mars-Pluto sesquisquare on **June 6** applies pressure that could provoke anger. Fortunately, gracious Venus forms a charming sextile with Mars, giving you the skills to avoid conflict or settle it amicably. These are passionate connections that can also express themselves through creative partnership or erotic attraction. Sweet talk and playful conversations make for a highly entertaining weekend as Mercury joins the party with a triple conjunction involving the Sun and Venus on **June 7-9**. Share this time with friendly folks who allow you to let your guard down and relax.

★ **JUNE 13-14**
escape reality
The Sun's square with electric Uranus on **June 13** may put you on edge with last-minute changes and interruptions in your schedule. A bright idea could help you find a way to stay loose, but so could a break in routine. A lazy

CAPRICORN 2008

Venus-Neptune trine is ideal for escaping reality with some frivolous shopping or by means of a romantic fantasy. However, don't jump into a new relationship on **June 14**, when Mars's conjunction with the karmic South Node of the Moon is likely to bring more fighting than fun. Still, a Sun-Neptune trine on the same day helps you to forgive, forget, and renew faith in yourself.

SUPER NOVA DAYS

★ **JUNE 18-20**
safe landing
Venus opposes Pluto for a last-minute emotional purge before slipping into caring Cancer and your 7th House of Relationships on **June 18**, opening you to the gentle support of a loved one who provides emotional nourishment to warm your life after the storm. A crispy Mars-Uranus quincunx very early on **June 19**, however, may temporarily interrupt the mellow mood with a fast-moving crisis. The drama may be greater than necessary, so avoid impulsive reactions that only add fuel to the fire. Mercury's direct turn permits everything

that's been on hold to finally start flowing again. The Sun opposes threatening Pluto on **June 20** before entering protective Cancer—the turning point of the Summer Solstice. You may feel as if you're struggling against a dangerous riptide before you finally land safely on the beach.

★ **JUNE 25–26**
strategic review
The Sun's smooth sextile with practical Saturn on **June 25** earns you respect, yet an idealistic Venus-Neptune sesquisquare can blind your judgment about others. Be kind, but don't give away more than you can afford. A Jupiter-Saturn sesquisquare on **June 26** may put a kink in your plans. This is a perfect time to review what you've done since this pair's first aspect on **March 18**, and to adjust your efforts before the last in the series on **January 30, 2009**.

JULY

JULY

A LITTLE HELP FROM YOUR FRIENDS

Deepening emotional connections with others remain a major theme in your life this month. Paradoxically, active Mars opens up new territory by moving into your 9th House of Faraway Places on **July 1** as the nurturing Cancer New Moon on **July 2** puts close relationships back into the spotlight. This Sun-Moon conjunction in your 7th House of Partnerships is joined by attractive Venus and opposed by expansive Jupiter, improving the quality and increasing the quantity of people in your life. A tendency to overestimate others is possible, but it's important to take the risk of putting your personal feelings and professional ideas out there, where they are likely to be well received. Talkative Mercury enters your 7th House on **July 10**, opening even more lines of communication and encouraging you with validating information. A heavy-duty Mars-Saturn conjunction the same day, however, can present you with some very clear restrictions or duties that slow you down. Patience and practicality are essential under these demanding circumstances.

CAPRICORN 2008

Your normally reserved emotions may spill over during the Full Moon in your sign on **July 18**. If insecurities surface, it's not an indication that all is lost, but simply a chance to highlight personal issues that need extra attention. Health and vitality may be at the top of the list, so make sure you get proper nutrition and exercise to deal with your daily stress. The Sun's entry into Leo in your 8th House of Intimacy on **July 22**, followed by Mercury on **July 26**, raises the stakes in relationships. If you're willing to give more of yourself, the rewards could be priceless. It's time to open up your heart and make your pitch for the emotional or material support necessary to bring you more happiness.

KEEP IN MIND THIS MONTH

Instead of stoically driving yourself forward without complaint, asking for assistance invites others in and makes your life much easier.

JULY

KEY DATES

★ **JULY 2-4**
great expectations
The super-sweet Cancer New Moon on **July 2** is ideal for sharing joy with others. But an opposition between indulgent Venus and excessive Jupiter on **July 3** can stretch hopes beyond reason. Avoid overspending or putting your faith in promises that cannot be kept. You don't need to be cynical; just temper optimism with a dash of reality to keep your feet on the ground. In any case, serious Saturn's testing semisquare with Venus on **July 4** will put the brakes on runaway expectations by confronting you with the practical limits of the here and now.

SUPER NOVA DAYS

★ **JULY 9-10**
save your strength
You may be ready for a big move personally or professionally on **July 9**, when the Sun opposes Jupiter in ambitious Capricorn. But if it puts more responsibility on your shoulders, make sure you have a solid support system in place.

CAPRICORN 2008

This expansive impulse encounters some very down-to-earth demands with a no-nonsense Mars-Saturn conjunction and a sharp-eyed Mercury-Pluto opposition on **July 10**. Both help you narrow your focus and concentrate on one task at a time. Don't waste these precious resources on protracted struggles when you can do your own groundbreaking work right now.

★ **JULY 14–15**
intuitive powers
An intelligent Mercury-Saturn sextile and an inventive Sun-Uranus trine on **July 14** show you angles that others can't see. Share your insights discreetly, since announcing them publicly could be embarrassing to a person in authority. Mercury hooks up smartly with active Mars on **July 15** and then slips on a sesquisquare with Neptune while the Sun clashes with the warrior planet and quincunxes illusory Neptune. Your mind may shift in and out of focus, and actions could be uncertain. Still, if you're receptive to feedback, you can make subtle adjustments that maintain your dignity and keep your efforts on track.

JULY

★ JULY 22
back to basics

The Sun's entry into proud Leo could bring an arrogant person into your life. Display your confidence, but don't get into a showdown: A sticky Mercury-Saturn semisquare can bog you down in petty details that distract from the big picture. Stick to the facts and keep conversations simple to make your point without making waves.

★ JULY 26
passion play

Mercury enters showy Leo and forms a testy semisquare with fiery Mars as it trines enthusiastic Jupiter. The first aspect spurs fast thinking, while the second increases your sense of adventure. This is excellent for play, passion, and romance, but the sheer force of your personality can overpower the meek. Controlling your excitement doesn't mean suppressing it, but rather intentionally redirecting it to produce the desired results.

AUGUST

AUGUST

SETTLING ACCOUNTS

This amazing month has two New Moons and two eclipses that indicate significant shifts in your life. The Leo New Moon Eclipse on **August 1** is in your 8th House of Shared Resources, altering the dynamics of a financial partnership or possibly an intimate relationship. You may suddenly discover that previous promises are not as solid as you thought, and you may wish to withdraw from a commitment. Either way, it's vital to discuss these issues openly. Show the courage to express your needs and be honest about what you are willing to give in return. This straightforward approach is your best guarantee for reinforcing a connection you want to keep or setting yourself on a path to establishing more fulfilling ones. The intelligent Aquarius Full Moon Eclipse on **August 16** is in your 2nd House of Income, generating changes in your revenue stream. Dreamy Neptune conjunct the eclipse tempts you to pursue financial fantasies, or extracts a price if you've already done so. At its best, this event can inspire you to develop your talent in creative new ways, but monetary restraint is recommended no matter what.

CAPRICORN 2008

The meticulous Virgo New Moon on **August 30** joins businesslike Saturn in your 9th House of Higher Thought and Faraway Places. Traveling with a purpose is smart, but you could find a leisure trip complicated by delays or cancellations. This lunation also reveals the need for specialized training to advance your career or for personal growth. You typically learn more within a clearly defined, hands-on education than by studying abstract ideas or theories. Mastering new material can be slow at first, but the skills you develop are well worth the time invested.

KEEP IN MIND THIS MONTH

You can't control the course of a relationship all by yourself—not even with compromise and communication. It takes two to make a partnership work.

AUGUST

KEY DATES

★ AUGUST 6
permission to wander

Venus moves into fussy Virgo where she likes everything neat and orderly, but none of the other planets want to fall in line. A voracious Sun-Jupiter quincunx leads to overdoing and overpromising, and a Mars-Uranus opposition is too impulsive and independent to follow any rules. Your mind won't cooperate, either, with a muddy Mercury-Neptune opposition that fuzzes facts with vague feelings. So relax and enjoy this creative, imaginative, and unconventional environment instead of demanding that you or anyone else stays on point or sticks to a schedule.

SUPER NOVA DAYS

★ AUGUST 13-16
flexibility works

You may be very sensitive to criticism as evaluative Venus joins with rigid Saturn on **August 13**. If you aren't getting the approval you desire, or others disappoint you, don't take it hard—it's all too easy right now to see things in a negative light. The Sun's unsettling quincunx with eccentric Uranus on **August 14** can shake up your routine, and your confidence. Stay light on your feet and adapt to changes rather than getting caught up in a battle over authority. This easygoing attitude will also serve you well on **August 15**, since the Sun's opposition to squishy Neptune may have other people bailing out on their responsibilities. A mentally tough Mercury-Saturn conjunction has you looking for solid answers, but if you try to pin people down, they will probably come up with sob stories or weak excuses. The tension breaks on **August 16** with a generous Venus-Jupiter trine that encourages you to spend your money and time on pleasure.

★ **AUGUST 22-23**
change of tune
The Sun's entry into fellow earth sign Virgo on **August 22** helps put you at your practical and strategic best. Your ability to handle details without losing sight of the big picture makes you an effective leader and planner. The tone is

AUGUST

very different, though, on **August 23** when Mercury and Venus oppose volatile Uranus. This is a day of surprises that's best taken with a sense of humor and a willingness to change directions at a moment's notice.

★ AUGUST 27–30
the naked truth

Mercury forms a hard-edged square with secretive Pluto on **August 27** that is likely to intensify all communications. The mental planet's shift into fair-minded Libra on **August 28** would normally lift the dark mood, but Venus squares Pluto on **August 29**, keeping suspicion and mistrust in the air. Finally, on **August 30**, gracious Venus enters her peaceful home sign of Libra. Now you can let go of recent wounds and begin the process of healing and reconciliation.

SEPTEMBER

SEPTEMBER ♑

ON-THE-JOB DIPLOMACY

This month is a key time of transition as visionary Jupiter turns direct in ambitious Capricorn on **September 8**. The forward movement of the planet of opportunity advances plans that have been brewing under the surface for the past few months. This Jupiter station is exceptionally powerful, because the giant planet forms a constructive trine with solid Saturn as it changes direction. The cooperative alignment of these two worldly planets cultivates solid ground that should bear fruit when their long series of aspects ends on **November 21**. The Full Moon in imaginative Pisces on **September 15** can bring surprises to your daily life and send your thinking in a new direction. Its conjunction with eccentric Uranus in your 3rd House of Information sparks your intuition and interest in unusual subjects, but can also lead to strange conversations or sudden breakdowns in communication.

The Sun enters diplomatic Libra and your 10th House of Career on **September 22**, emphasizing your professional life—especially how you connect with your colleagues. You'll gain insights, but it

CAPRICORN 2008

may take time to implement them, because Mercury turns retrograde on **September 24**. This three-week reversal of the messenger planet in your 10th House requires greater care in how you share information on the job. Miscommunication can cause conflict, so speak clearly and directly to head off potential trouble. Bright ideas work best when you think through all of their ramifications before revealing them to others. The New Moon in Libra on **September 29** is square Jupiter in your sign, convincing you to seek more responsibility in your current position or consider looking for greener pastures. Who you know now is as important as what you know, so shore up your alliances before making a major move.

KEEP IN MIND THIS MONTH

Responding to the needs and desires of other people will help you enlist their cooperation—as well as promoting your own ambitions.

SEPTEMBER   ♑

KEY DATES

★ **SEPTEMBER 3-4**
your future is calling
The Sun joins your ruling planet, Saturn, on **September 3**, which is often a time for slowing down and taking stock of your life. The potential for frustration is limited, though, since the creative Sun is on its way to a generous trine with boundless Jupiter on **September 4**. This might feel like a trip from a tiny closet to the great outdoors, but it's actually a preview of the life-shaping trine between Jupiter and Saturn on **September 8**. Here's your chance to glimpse the future and to give it a nudge in the direction you want it to go.

SUPER NOVA DAYS

★ **SEPTEMBER 7-8**
strategic commitment
Energetic Mars squares overenthusiastic Jupiter on **September 7**, which might stretch your resources too thin. You could see a small dispute grow into a major battle, or a little task into a giant chore. Narrow your focus to harness

CAPRICORN 2008

the power you're feeling now and channel it more judiciously in the days ahead. Jupiter's direct turn and positive trine with Saturn on **September 8** give you a perfect balance between high hopes and down-to-earth common sense. You can apply your force effectively to bring about long-term changes. Intense Pluto is also shifting into forward gear, showing that you are ready to express your deepest desires in a constructive manner.

★ SEPTEMBER 14–15
skillful adaptation

A socially skillful Mercury-Venus conjunction on **September 14** makes you a delightful communicator. Creative ideas flow in a friendly manner that entertains as well as informs. This peaceful mood may pass on **September 15**, however, when the Full Moon's emotional high tides are intensified by the presence of wild Uranus. Stay alert to catch unexpected waves of inspiration and avoid being blindsided by unexpected news.

SEPTEMBER

★ SEPTEMBER 20–22
tough and tender
A stressful Sun-Pluto square on **September 20** spawns power struggles and difficulties in sharing authority, but at least it finally brings deeper issues out into the open. Fortunately, a sweet Mars-Neptune trine on **September 21** softens conflict and turns a potential tug-of-war into a playful pillow fight. The Sun enters harmonious Libra on **September 22**, the Autumn Equinox, for a last-minute evaluation of relationships two days before Mercury goes retrograde when serious negotiations should be shelved.

★ SEPTEMBER 28
quick-change artist
A jumpy Venus-Uranus sesquisquare may upset your social plans. Even your most reliable friends could fail to follow through on commitments, but the possibility of meeting someone new could make up for it. Besides, you're ready for fresh ways to play, and an easygoing Mercury-Neptune trine allows you to be more relaxed and less concerned about the rules.

OCTOBER

OCTOBER ♑

BUILDING A TEAM

The month starts with a highly focused Mars-Pluto sextile on **October 1**, pushing you toward greater efficiency when working as part of a team. When active Mars enters your 11th House of Groups on **October 4**, your innate drive for productivity increases. This could trigger your competitive streak or a battle of wills, even with your closest friends. Balancing your desire to get work done quickly with a gentle touch ensures that peace and harmony are maintained during these intense times. The relationship between independent action and compromise is highlighted by the rowdy Aries Full Moon on **October 14**. This fiery lunar event occurs in your 4th House of Roots, perhaps stimulating an impulse to go it alone. Stress at home can cause impatient reactions that you might regret. Rapidly rising feelings reveal where you feel constrained by compromise, yet their purpose is to stimulate further contemplation rather than immediate action.

Mercury the Messenger turns direct on **October 15** in your 10th House of Career, enabling you to move on ideas stirred during the previous three weeks. Yet the impatience of the Aries Full Moon still burns inside you, so weigh the impact of your words before making provocative statements. With your methodical nature, you feel more comfortable with the Sun's entry into the water sign Scorpio on **October 22**; its intensity forces you to deeply examine your surroundings before making a move. The relentless Scorpio New Moon on **October 28** in your social 11th House quietly feeds your ambition as you recognize the untapped resources around you. Combining your efforts with others makes it possible to transform organizations, resurrect discarded projects, or produce events that powerfully impact your community.

KEEP IN MIND THIS MONTH

Even if your efforts have failed in the past, you can do things differently this time and enjoy a rousing success.

KEY DATES

SUPER NOVA DAYS

★ **OCTOBER 5–7**
return to reason
A semisquare from immovable Saturn on **October 5** slows down assertive Mars, reminding you not to work so hard. Resist the pressure of a pushy pal, especially with a Venus-Pluto semisquare that may make you feel indebted to this person. If you want to give, do it voluntarily; coercion will only elicit resentment. Fortunately, a hopeful Venus-Jupiter sextile can bring a happy ending to even the most contentious interaction. Retrograde Mercury joins the Sun on **October 6** as both form excessive squares with Jupiter. This could produce an "eureka" moment when a long-standing mystery is solved. Just give yourself time to think it through, Capricorn, Jupiter loves jumping to conclusions. On **October 7,** a stabilizing Venus-Saturn sextile restores reason and restraint, contributing to sound judgment and more solid relationships.

★ OCTOBER 11
let go
Venus in emotionally powerful Scorpio squares diffusive Neptune in Aquarius, which can leave you confusing a dream with reality; spend your love and money cautiously. You are gifted now with compassion and inspiration, empowering you to heal even the harshest of wounds and helping you let go of the past.

★ OCTOBER 17-18
inner quest
Relationship repairs are in order on **October 17** when a brilliant Venus-Saturn quintile helps you create joy even under difficult circumstances. You can earn recognition from someone who has been unable to appreciate your talent in the past. When Venus fires into adventurous Sagittarius and semisquares extravagant Jupiter on **October 18**, you uncharacteristically leave caution behind as you pursue love and pleasure. What you seek may be more spiritual than material; fulfilling your quest may be about looking within, not chasing someone or something outside yourself.

OCTOBER

★ OCTOBER 25
out in the open
Competition may create friction as a tense Sun-Saturn semisquare encourages a struggle for control. Aggressive Mars squares the karmic Lunar Nodes, sharpening edges that make compromise more difficult. While you may feel uncomfortable with an honest difference of opinion, the tension will pass more quickly than if you deny your personal truth.

★ OCTOBER 27–30
beyond smoke and mirrors
A friction-free sextile between mobile Mars and buoyant Jupiter enriches you with energy on **October 28**. The encouragement of a spirited partner is there to back you up, but Mercury caroms off crazy Uranus with a quincunx that complicates conversations. Fortunately, the communication planet's healing trine with understanding Neptune on **October 30** can fill in the gaps with feelings when the words aren't clear. A strong Mars-Saturn sextile helps you attract reliable assistance to get your work done more efficiently.

NOVEMBER

NOVEMBER

IRREPRESSIBLE CHANGE

The month begins with a powerful Saturn-Uranus opposition on **November 8** that will return four more times during the next two years. This face-off between orderly Saturn in Virgo and revolutionary Uranus in Pisces across your educational 3rd and 9th Houses can leave you restructuring your entire worldview. Saturn in your 9th House of Higher Truth corresponds with a need to prove your beliefs in concrete terms, but intuitive Uranus in the 3rd House of Immediate Environment opens your mind with inexplicable ideas and exceptions to your intellectual rules. You're likely to question authority—even the very nature of reality—but there's no need to resolve these issues right now. This long-term aspect gives you plenty of time to explore the many contradictions you may experience first.

All-embracing Jupiter helps you make room for living both in the familiar world of reality and in a new and exciting world of wonder by forming harmonious aspects to Uranus and Saturn this month. Jupiter forms its third and final sextile to Uranus on **November 13** to advance bright ideas

CAPRICORN 2008

and breakthroughs that originated in late March and May. Jupiter makes its last trine with Saturn on **November 21** in a series that began on **March 16, 2007**. This creative balance between optimism and practicality gives you a solid foundation for professional and spiritual growth. The planet that can tie all these pieces together is penetrating, pressurized Pluto, which reenters Capricorn on **November 26** for a fifteen-year stay after its brief retrograde retreat into Sagittarius. Pluto has the power to squeeze out what you no longer need to direct your life in a more purposeful way. You have already made some significant changes, but these may just be preparation for bigger ones yet to come.

KEEP IN MIND THIS MONTH

It is reasonable to feel secure in some ways and uncertain in others. You don't need to be a superhero to achieve your goals.

NOVEMBER ♑

KEY DATES

★ **NOVEMBER 3-4**
wait out the storm
Venus squares Saturn and Uranus on **November 3**—one day before their exact opposition—creating confusion in relationships and personal values. Feelings can bounce from excitement to fear and back again, making commitment or clarity difficult. With pushy Mars square mushy Neptune on **November 4**, it's common to waste energy and fight the wrong battles; doing less is the wise choice. Mental Mercury's move into perceptive Scorpio the same day is bound to reveal a secret or two, indicating that you will soon have more information upon which to make a decision.

SUPER NOVA DAYS

★ **NOVEMBER 10-13**
head over heart
The Sun's positive aspects with Jupiter and Uranus on **November 10** bring you hope and originality, perhaps with the aid of a friend or colleague. The Sun's sextile with Saturn on

November 11 supports you with competence and quiet confidence. However, an intense Venus-Pluto conjunction in your 12th House of Secrets on **November 12** can rouse distrust with others that undermines relationships. Venus then enters your sign, giving you clarity to address this issue and reestablish a healthy bond. The sensual Taurus Full Moon on **November 13** falls in your romantic 5th House in opposition to passionate Mars but square unrealistic Neptune. Powerful feelings of desire may provoke foolish action. Let your head lead the way, and your heart can follow safely.

★ **NOVEMBER 16**
journey within
Intellectual Mercury gets even smarter with harmonious aspects to Jupiter, Saturn, and Uranus. This brilliant trio of vision, logic, and originality empowers your ideas and makes you an engaging conversationalist. Yet with active Mars entering adventurous Sagittarius in your 12th House of Privacy, you might be more interested in taking a long walk by yourself than chatting the day away with others.

NOVEMBER

★ NOVEMBER 21
guiding light

The Sun slingshots into Sagittarius as its ruling planet, Jupiter, trines Saturn, allowing you to peer far into the future. You may feel guided by a higher power, but it's really your own awareness that's expanding to show you a clear connection between where you are now and where you're going next.

★ NOVEMBER 27–29
practice self-restraint

The New Moon in extroverted Sagittarius on **November 27** occurs as brilliant Uranus turns direct, giving you a double dose of intuition and inspiration. You may be excited by your discoveries and anxious to share the news, but it's not for everyone's ears. Following a gossipy Mercury-Mars conjunction on **November 28** that urges you to spill the beans, a discreet Venus-Saturn trine on **November 29** brings maturity and tact to help you gain control over your impulses.

DECEMBER

DECEMBER ♑

SEASON OF RENEWAL

Vivacious Venus enters unconventional Aquarius and your 2nd House of Resources on **December 7**, putting you in a spending mood just in time for the holidays. Your taste could be a little unusual this year, which is fine for you, but it also might tempt you to buy some strange gifts. The airy Gemini Full Moon on **December 12** is especially intense with militant Mars in opposition while strict Saturn and rebellious Uranus make challenging squares. This jittery event occurs in your 6th House of Employment, which could produce a crisis on the job. The additional pressure of unpleasant colleagues or an unexpected shift of duties could trigger your desire to seek greener pastures. Yet even if another opportunity opens up, conditions are so volatile now that it's better to carefully consider all the angles than to suddenly make a change.

The Sun's entry into traditional Capricorn on **December 21** marks the Winter Solstice and a return to longer days in the Northern Hemisphere. The uplifting potential of this event is temporarily delayed as the Sun passes over mysterious Pluto

CAPRICORN 2008

on **December 22**. This conjunction may plunge you into complete self-examination that focuses on your deepest desires. If they seem achievable to you, this transit can empower and propel you toward them. Yet if what you want most seems impossible to reach, you could feel desperate. Happily, industrious Mars enters Capricorn on **December 27** to invigorate you hours before the New Moon in your sign, giving you hope for a better tomorrow. Mars's passage over Pluto on **December 28** reveals hidden reserves of energy and willpower, motivating you to take on any challenge and giving you the strength to come out on top.

KEEP IN MIND THIS MONTH

Instead of just working hard out of habit, stop and consolidate your resources for a climb to heights you've never reached before.

DECEMBER

KEY DATES

★ **DECEMBER 5-6**
rapid response
An early-morning Mercury-Uranus square on **December 5** speeds up your thinking and speech. This is great if you have a creative way to apply your ideas—a Sun-Mars conjunction the same day tends to incite fast and furious reactions. Applying this punch productively is clearly more desirable than lashing out in frustration. In addition, a testing Mercury-Saturn square on **December 6** is a sobering reminder of responsibility. Thoughtful strategic actions will earn you respect, but careless ones can bring regret.

SUPER NOVA DAY

★ **DECEMBER 12**
many directions at once
The supercharged Full Moon in multifaceted Gemini combines active and impatient Mars and Uranus with serious Saturn, making this an "emotional earthquake" day. If you're feeling dazed and confused, don't struggle to control

CAPRICORN 2008

the situation. It's best to be as flexible as you can when buffeted by wildly fluctuating feelings inside and suddenly changing events outside. The upside is that all this activity can wake up new insights, shake out bad habits, and inspire you to try an unorthodox approach to your work.

★ DECEMBER 15
the right stuff
Speedy Mars and slowpoke Saturn hook up in a tense square, demanding that you follow the letter of the law. A reckless friend or colleague might encourage you to cut corners or make a questionable claim, but even if they get away with it, you have a good chance of getting caught. Integrity is essential since your willingness to face facts and do things the right way—even if it's the hard way—will not only keep you out of trouble but actually save you time and effort in the long run.

★ DECEMBER 21–22
all or nothing
You deserve recognition for your ongoing efforts with the Sun's entry into your sign on

DECEMBER   ♑

December 21. However, a jealous Venus-Pluto semisquare may reduce the appreciation others show you now. A fearful or controlling person could make relationships less satisfying—or perhaps one of you expresses needs the other just won't meet. The Sun's conjunction with Pluto on **December 22** could bring things to a head with a threat to sever your connection. The real issue is whether you value this relationship enough to dig in, face your own doubts, and do what you must to make it work.

★ **DECEMBER 27**
the dance of love
The New Moon in dedicated Capricorn arrives as Warrior Mars enters your sign, which should toughen your resolve, but lovable Venus joining sensitive Neptune matches strength with vulnerability. Knowing when to lead and when to follow ideally creates a delicious combination of physical desire and romantic openness.

APPENDIXES

★

2008 MONTH-AT-A-GLANCE ASTROCALENDAR

★

FAMOUS CAPRICORNS

★

CAPRICORN IN LOVE

JANUARY 2008

TUESDAY 1	
WEDNESDAY 2	
THURSDAY 3	
FRIDAY 4	
SATURDAY 5	

SUNDAY 6 ★ Tough love has meaningful and lasting effects

MONDAY 7	
TUESDAY 8	
WEDNESDAY 9	
THURSDAY 10	
FRIDAY 11	
SATURDAY 12	

SUNDAY 13 ★ Settle for shortcuts in communication through the 14th

MONDAY 14 ★	
TUESDAY 15	
WEDNESDAY 16	
THURSDAY 17	
FRIDAY 18	
SATURDAY 19	

SUNDAY 20 ★ Embrace an unorthodox approach through the 21st

MONDAY 21 ★	
TUESDAY 22	
WEDNESDAY 23	

THURSDAY 24 ★ **SUPER NOVA DAYS** Make room for new love through the 25th

FRIDAY 25 ★	
SATURDAY 26	
SUNDAY 27	
MONDAY 28	

TUESDAY 29 ★ Relationships find a more solid footing through the 30th

WEDNESDAY 30 ★	
THURSDAY 31	

FEBRUARY 2008

FRIDAY 1 ★ Prior efforts bring sweet rewards today

SATURDAY 2
SUNDAY 3
MONDAY 4
TUESDAY 5
WEDNESDAY 6 ★ Play with your style and social life without consequences now

---

THURSDAY 7 ★
FRIDAY 8
SATURDAY 9
SUNDAY 10
MONDAY 11
TUESDAY 12
WEDNESDAY 13 ★ A clash of styles stirs a romantic realignment through the 14th

---

THURSDAY 14 ★
FRIDAY 15
SATURDAY 16
SUNDAY 17
MONDAY 18
TUESDAY 19
WEDNESDAY 20 ★ **SUPER NOVA DAYS**
    Delay gratification when duty calls through the 21st

THURSDAY 21 ★
FRIDAY 22
SATURDAY 23
    SUNDAY 24 ★ Commit your limited resources with care

MONDAY 25
TUESDAY 26
WEDNESDAY 27
THURSDAY 28
FRIDAY 29

MARCH 2008

SATURDAY 1

SUNDAY 2

MONDAY 3

TUESDAY 4 ★ Today is the day to make your move in a relationship or project

WEDNESDAY 5

THURSDAY 6

FRIDAY 7 ★ **SUPER NOVA DAYS**
Make a major change or else give up through the 8th

SATURDAY 8 ★

SUNDAY 9

MONDAY 10

TUESDAY 11

WEDNESDAY 12

THURSDAY 13

FRIDAY 14 ★ Recognize your source of dissatisfaction through the 15th

SATURDAY 15 ★

SUNDAY 16

MONDAY 17

TUESDAY 18

WEDNESDAY 19

THURSDAY 20

FRIDAY 21 ★ Be confident before burning bridges through the 23rd

SATURDAY 22 ★

SUNDAY 23 ★

MONDAY 24

TUESDAY 25

WEDNESDAY 26

THURSDAY 27 ★ Break your own rules to increase pleasure through the 28th

FRIDAY 28 ★

SATURDAY 29

SUNDAY 30

MONDAY 31

APRIL 2008

TUESDAY 1

WEDNESDAY 2

THURSDAY 3

FRIDAY 4

SATURDAY 5

SUNDAY 6 ★ A timely intervention now keeps a situation from getting messy

MONDAY 7

TUESDAY 8

WEDNESDAY 9

THURSDAY 10 ★ Stick close to the facts in order to grow

FRIDAY 11 ★

SATURDAY 12

SUNDAY 13

MONDAY 14 ★ Don't take it personally if your efforts are thwarted

TUESDAY 15

WEDNESDAY 16

THURSDAY 17

FRIDAY 18 ★ Satisfy yourself through the 19th and others will appreciate it later

SATURDAY 19 ★

SUNDAY 20

MONDAY 21 ★ **SUPER NOVA DAYS** Ride a wave of passion through the 24th

TUESDAY 22 ★

WEDNESDAY 23 ★

THURSDAY 24 ★

FRIDAY 25

SATURDAY 26

SUNDAY 27

MONDAY 28

TUESDAY 29

WEDNESDAY 30

MAY 2008

THURSDAY 1 ★ Get down to business! Cut to the chase through the 3rd

---

FRIDAY 2 ★
SATURDAY 3 ★
SUNDAY 4
MONDAY 5
TUESDAY 6
WEDNESDAY 7
THURSDAY 8
FRIDAY 9 ★ Bring a creative enterprise to life through the 12th

---

SATURDAY 10 ★
SUNDAY 11 ★
MONDAY 12 ★
TUESDAY 13
WEDNESDAY 14
THURSDAY 15
FRIDAY 16
SATURDAY 17
SUNDAY 18 ★ Share your boundless joy with loved ones

MONDAY 19
TUESDAY 20 ★ **SUPER NOVA DAYS** Create new rules through the 22nd

---

WEDNESDAY 21 ★
THURSDAY 22 ★
FRIDAY 23
SATURDAY 24
SUNDAY 25
MONDAY 26 ★ Self-assessment now will eventually lead to greater rewards

---

TUESDAY 27
WEDNESDAY 28
THURSDAY 29
FRIDAY 30
SATURDAY 31

JUNE 2008

SUNDAY 1	
MONDAY 2	
TUESDAY 3	
WEDNESDAY 4	
THURSDAY 5	
FRIDAY 6 ★	Let your guard down. It's time to play through the 9th

SATURDAY 7 ★	
SUNDAY 8 ★	
MONDAY 9 ★	
TUESDAY 10	
WEDNESDAY 11	
THURSDAY 12	
FRIDAY 13 ★	Escape into frivolity or romantic fantasy through the 14th

SATURDAY 14 ★	
SUNDAY 15	
MONDAY 16	
TUESDAY 17	
WEDNESDAY 18 ★	**SUPER NOVA DAYS** Find safe landing after a storm through the 20th

THURSDAY 19 ★	
FRIDAY 20 ★	
SATURDAY 21	
SUNDAY 22	
MONDAY 23	
TUESDAY 24	
WEDNESDAY 25 ★	Review your actions and adjust your efforts through the 26th

THURSDAY 26 ★	
FRIDAY 27	
SATURDAY 28	
SUNDAY 29	
MONDAY 30	

JULY 2008

TUESDAY 1

WEDNESDAY 2 ★ Practical limits trump great expectations through the 4th

THURSDAY 3 ★

FRIDAY 4 ★

SATURDAY 5

SUNDAY 6

MONDAY 7

TUESDAY 8

WEDNESDAY 9 ★ **SUPER NOVA DAYS** Save your strength through the 10th

THURSDAY 10 ★

FRIDAY 11

SATURDAY 12

SUNDAY 13

MONDAY 14 ★ Use your intuitive powers discreetly through the 15th

TUESDAY 15 ★

WEDNESDAY 16

THURSDAY 17

FRIDAY 18

SATURDAY 19

SUNDAY 20

MONDAY 21

TUESDAY 22 ★ Get back to basics when petty details bog you down

WEDNESDAY 23

THURSDAY 24

FRIDAY 25

SATURDAY 26 ★ Redirect your passion to produce desired results

SUNDAY 27

MONDAY 28

TUESDAY 29

WEDNESDAY 30

THURSDAY 31

AUGUST 2008

FRIDAY 1
SATURDAY 2
SUNDAY 3
MONDAY 4
TUESDAY 5
WEDNESDAY 6 ★ Give yourself permission to be imaginative and unconventional

THURSDAY 7
FRIDAY 8
SATURDAY 9
SUNDAY 10
MONDAY 11
TUESDAY 12
WEDNESDAY 13 ★ **SUPER NOVA DAYS** Flexibility is key through the 16th

THURSDAY 14 ★
FRIDAY 15 ★
SATURDAY 16 ★
SUNDAY 17
MONDAY 18
TUESDAY 19
WEDNESDAY 20
THURSDAY 21
FRIDAY 22 ★ A change of tune requires a sense of humor through the 23rd

SATURDAY 23 ★
SUNDAY 24
MONDAY 25
TUESDAY 26
WEDNESDAY 27 ★ Intense communications reveal the naked truth through the 30th

THURSDAY 28 ★
FRIDAY 29 ★
SATURDAY 30 ★
SUNDAY 31

SEPTEMBER 2008

MONDAY 1	
TUESDAY 2	
WEDNESDAY 3 ★	Slow down to take stock—your future is calling now

THURSDAY 4 ★	
FRIDAY 5	
SATURDAY 6	
SUNDAY 7 ★	**SUPER NOVA DAYS** Make only strategic commitments through the 8th

MONDAY 8 ★	
TUESDAY 9	
WEDNESDAY 10	
THURSDAY 11	
FRIDAY 12	
SATURDAY 13	
SUNDAY 14 ★	You adapt skillfully to unexpected news through the 15th

MONDAY 15 ★	
TUESDAY 16	
WEDNESDAY 17	
THURSDAY 18	
FRIDAY 19	
SATURDAY 20 ★	Work out tough and tender issues through the 22nd

SUNDAY 21 ★	
MONDAY 22 ★	
TUESDAY 23	
WEDNESDAY 24	
THURSDAY 25	
FRIDAY 26	
SATURDAY 27	
SUNDAY 28 ★	Stay relaxed to have fun when social plans are up in the air

MONDAY 29	
TUESDAY 30	

OCTOBER 2008

| WEDNESDAY 1 |
| THURSDAY 2 |
| FRIDAY 3 |
| SATURDAY 4 |
| SUNDAY 5 ★ **SUPER NOVA DAYS** Return to reason through the 7th |

| MONDAY 6 ★ |
| TUESDAY 7 ★ |
| WEDNESDAY 8 |
| THURSDAY 9 |
| FRIDAY 10 |
| SATURDAY 11 ★ Let go of the past to heal even the harshest of wounds |

| SUNDAY 12 |
| MONDAY 13 |
| TUESDAY 14 |
| WEDNESDAY 15 |
| THURSDAY 16 |
| FRIDAY 17 ★ Focus your quest inward through the 18th |

| SATURDAY 18 ★ |
| SUNDAY 19 |
| MONDAY 20 |
| TUESDAY 21 |
| WEDNESDAY 22 |
| THURSDAY 23 |
| FRIDAY 24 |
| SATURDAY 25 ★ Tension passes quickly when it's out in the open |

| SUNDAY 26 |
| MONDAY 27 |
| TUESDAY 28 ★ Trust your feelings when words aren't clear through the 30th |

| WEDNESDAY 29 ★ |
| THURSDAY 30 ★ |
| FRIDAY 31 |

NOVEMBER 2008

SATURDAY 1

SUNDAY 2

MONDAY 3 ★ Wait out the storm of shifting feelings through the 4th

TUESDAY 4 ★

WEDNESDAY 5

THURSDAY 6

FRIDAY 7

SATURDAY 8

SUNDAY 9

MONDAY 10

TUESDAY 11 ☼ **SUPER NOVA DAYS**
Trust your head over your heart through the 13th

WEDNESDAY 12 ★

THURSDAY 13 ★

FRIDAY 14

SATURDAY 15

SUNDAY 16 ★ Vision, logic, and originality empower your ideas

MONDAY 17

TUESDAY 18

WEDNESDAY 19

THURSDAY 20

FRIDAY 21 ★ Your awareness is a guiding light to your objective

SATURDAY 22

SUNDAY 23

MONDAY 24

TUESDAY 25

WEDNESDAY 26

THURSDAY 27 ★ Practice restraint when you want to blab through the 29th

FRIDAY 28 ★

SATURDAY 29 ★

SUNDAY 30

DECEMBER 2008

MONDAY 1

TUESDAY 2

WEDNESDAY 3

THURSDAY 4

FRIDAY 5 ★ Find a creative way to apply your ideas through the 6th

SATURDAY 6 ★

SUNDAY 7

MONDAY 8

TUESDAY 9

WEDNESDAY 10

THURSDAY 11

FRIDAY 12 ★ **SUPER NOVA DAY** Stay flexible when feelings fluctuate

SATURDAY 13

SUNDAY 14

MONDAY 15 ★ Integrity is essential, saving time and effort in the long run

TUESDAY 16

WEDNESDAY 17

THURSDAY 18

FRIDAY 19

SATURDAY 20

SUNDAY 21 ★ Give all or nothing in relationships through the 22nd

MONDAY 22 ★

TUESDAY 23

WEDNESDAY 24

THURSDAY 25

FRIDAY 26

SATURDAY 27 ★ Learn when to lead and follow in the dance of love

SUNDAY 28

MONDAY 29

TUESDAY 30

WEDNESDAY 31

FAMOUS CAPRICORNS

Diane Sawyer	★	12/22/1945
Susan Lucci	★	12/23/1947
Howard Hughes	★	12/24/1905
Mary Higgins Clark	★	12/24/1929
Ava Gardner	★	12/24/1922
Humphrey Bogart	★	12/25/1899
Clara Barton	★	12/25/1821
Sir Isaac Newton	★	12/25/1642
Rickey Henderson	★	12/25/1958
Sissy Spacek	★	12/25/1949
Mao Tse-tung	★	12/26/1893
Phil Spector	★	12/26/1940
Marlene Dietrich	★	12/27/1901
Louis Pasteur	★	12/27/1822
Denzel Washington	★	12/28/1954
Mary Tyler Moore	★	12/29/1936
Marianne Faithful	★	12/29/1946
Jude Law	★	12/29/1972
Laila Ali	★	12/30/1977
Bo Diddly	★	12/30/1928
Patti Smith	★	12/30/1946
Rudyard Kipling	★	12/30/1865
Tiger Woods	★	12/30/1975
Matt Lauer	★	12/30/1957
Donna Summer	★	12/31/1948
Anthony Hopkins	★	12/31/1937
John Denver	★	12/31/1943
Henri Matisse	★	12/31/1869
Betsy Ross	★	1/1/1752
J. D. Salinger	★	1/1/1919
Cuba Gooding, Jr.	★	1/2/1968
Marion Davies	★	1/3/1897
Mel Gibson	★	1/3/1956
J. R. R. Tolkien	★	1/3/1892
Michael Stipe	★	1/4/1960
Louis Braille	★	1/4/1809

FAMOUS CAPRICORNS

Diane Keaton	★	1/5/1946
Robert Duvall	★	1/5/1931
Joan of Arc	★	1/6/1412
Katie Couric	★	1/7/1957
Nicolas Cage	★	1/7/1964
David Bowie	★	1/8/1947
Elvis Presley	★	1/8/1935
Joan Baez	★	1/9/1941
Richard Nixon	★	1/9/1913
Jimmy Page	★	1/9/1944
Dave Matthews	★	1/9/1967
Pat Benatar	★	1/10/1953
Jean Chrétien	★	1/11/1934
Howard Stern	★	1/12/1954
Rush Limbaugh	★	1/12/1951
Orlando Bloom	★	1/13/1977
Faye Dunaway	★	1/14/1941
LL Cool J	★	1/14/1968
Benedict Arnold	★	1/14/1741
Dr. Martin Luther King, Jr.	★	1/15/1929
Kate Moss	★	1/16/1974
Debbie Allen	★	1/16/1950
Jim Carrey	★	1/17/1962
Betty White	★	1/17/1922
Vidal Sassoon	★	1/17/1928
Muhammad Ali	★	1/17/1942
Eartha Kitt	★	1/17/1927
Al Capone	★	1/17/1899
Benjamin Franklin	★	1/17/1706
Cary Grant	★	1/18/1904
A. A. Milne	★	1/18/1882
Janis Joplin	★	1/19/1943
Edgar Allan Poe	★	1/19/1809
Robert E. Lee	★	1/19/1807
Dolly Parton	★	1/19/1946
Paul Cezanne	★	1/19/1839

CAPRICORN IN LOVE

CAPRICORN & ARIES (MARCH 21–APRIL 19)

You're cautious, responsible, and serious, and tend to hold back your feelings. You are also practical, preferring traditional and conservative friends and family circles. In a relationship, you're the stable one, willing to work on making it last. Being involved with a fiery Aries can be unnerving, as they're often very impulsive and will jump right into a job, project, or relationship without thinking it through first—which may seem childlike to you. You, on the other hand, make a plan, build your foundation, and then execute your plan accordingly. If, however, you have the Moon or Mars in a fire sign, you'll be ready to jump in and help, rather than scold them. Eventually your Aries lover may feel regularly thwarted by your stern eye. At the same time, you tire of feeling like you need to watch after him or her. But in love and marriage, your practical maturity can help your Aries mate take responsibility more seriously. And you have much to gain as he or she can spark up the boring routines in your world. This match works as long as you are willing to let go of control issues, allowing your mate enough room to feel like there is a balance of power.

CAPRICORN IN LOVE

CAPRICORN & TAURUS (APRIL 20–MAY 20)

On the surface, this seems like the proverbial match made in heaven. Bull's are also concerned with down-to-earth matters, although there are differences. You see life as a mountain and strive to overcome any obstacles that may prevent you from reaching the summit. To you, integrity and hard work ultimately create success. Your Taurus lover may be as determined, but success for them is not about reaching the top—it's about material security. While your lover may want to spend money on nice creature comforts, you worry about stability and would rather do with less when the sun is shining in order to be ready for a rainy day. Still, Taurus is a good partner for you, and shares many of your lifestyle values. However, while your sign is ruled by austere Saturn, your Taurus mate is more connected with Venus, the planet of sensual enjoyment. Yet if Venus in your chart is in fiery Sagittarius or eclectic Aquarius, you may also appreciate possessions. Romantically, you both can have strong sexual needs, and although somewhat conservative, can be quite expressive. You both adore old buildings set in natural surroundings and long-lasting virtues—metaphors for what you seek within this stable relationship.

CAPRICORN IN LOVE

CAPRICORN & GEMINI (MAY 21–JUNE 20)

You usually choose your words with consideration. You Goats can be closed and conservative, especially in the early stages of a relationship, with little desire to expose your emotional vulnerability. Geminis, on the other hand, are associated, or ruled by, the communication planet Mercury, and tend to be talkative and spontaneous with their words and ideas. They do have a tendency to be rational and mental in their approach to life—making them more attuned to your ways. But the differences in your day-to-day communication patterns can be too much to overcome to make this relationship work, unless your chart has the Moon or Mars in an air sign (Gemini, Libra, or Aquarius). Even with an airy Moon or Mars, you tend to be slow to share internal thoughts, while your partner seems to be clever and carefree. Allow for these basic differences, and your Gemini can open wide your doors of communication, paving a path to deeper meaning from interpersonal relationships and increased self-awareness. Meanwhile, your partner can benefit from the stability and security that you bring to the team. If your noisy Twin can learn how to tone down their chatter when you need quietness, it can be a workable union.

CAPRICORN IN LOVE

CAPRICORN & CANCER (JUNE 21–JULY 22)

When two of the 12 astrological signs are opposite each other on the zodiacal wheel, they act like mirrors, each reflecting traits that the other sign needs. Opposites attract, and many couples share sign oppositions. You tend to be conservative with your emotions, which can make you seem stern or strict. You're hard-working, and prefer to socialize with intelligent individuals who carry respect and status. Cancer's emotional constitution is nurturing, warm, and sensitive. You're drawn to the outer world of career and success; he or she is drawn to the inner worlds of home and family. Together, you can make quite a team, covering both ends of the spectrum. Your lover may have changeable moods and can display emotions more overtly than most signs. Additionally, if you have the Moon, Venus, or Mars in water signs, you'll be more able to meet your hard-shelled Crab in a softer manner. You'll both need to adjust to each other with delicate candor and awareness. You stand to learn the virtues of the feeling world, and Cancer can learn the value of objectivity so as not to overwhelm you with trivial insecurities. This is a powerful common match-up, offering plenty of growing room for both of you.

CAPRICORN & LEO (JULY 23–AUGUST 22)

You're practical and hard working with little interest in frivolous fanfare. When you meet Leos, you are inclined to question the ways they draw attention to themselves. They can seem to be overly dramatic and outwardly too expressive for your reserved tastes. The Lion's attitude can build barriers between you, for Leo needs and wants love that is demonstrative, tangible, and personal. You may lose patience with your mate's need for what seems like nearly constant approval and admiration. In the beginning of this union, your Leo lover may generously give affection and gifts to you, hoping for reciprocation and love in return. Later, as the relationship advances beyond the romantic stage, your Lion could be wounded by your lack of fiery romantic demonstration, and may pull away and sulk. He or she will need to come to grips with the fact that you are practical and levelheaded, and may not respond with the adoration that Leo wants. If you have Mars in a fire sign or if your Mercury is in Sagittarius, your chances for happiness with a Leo are greatly improved. If this relationship has a destiny, both of you must strive to be self-aware. You'll each need to give freely, even eagerly, to the other without expectation or demands.

CAPRICORN IN LOVE

CAPRICORN & VIRGO (AUGUST 23–SEPT. 22)

When two earth signs hook up, there is an immediate and basic similarity in the way you value things that are real, including jobs, financial responsibilities, and basic needs such as food and shelter. You remain committed and devoted to a task until it's finished. You cherish quality, honesty, and order. These attitudes toward life are compatible with your Virgo partner, who may be more service-oriented than you, but is also responsible, dutiful, and efficient. Together, you may enjoy studying, collecting, or gardening, and may share a fondness of nature and the outdoors. You enjoy achieving the goals you set out to attain, especially when you need to work hard to fulfill your dreams. Your Virgo mate is a consistent worker, who may not have your managerial skills, but who can attend to the details of a high-profile job or running a household. In a partnership, your Virgo can assist you greatly. If, however, the Moon or Mars in your chart is in Gemini or Pisces, you may find that sometimes you're working at cross-purposes. Together, you will move mountains as you pave your road into the future with logic and hard work. You can make a home that is practical and efficient, reflecting the nature of your mutual love.

CAPRICORN IN LOVE

CAPRICORN & LIBRA (SEPT. 23–OCT. 22)

You can do just about anything you put your mind to, and others can count on you for just about everything. Your weak point, however, is in the expressive realm, since you may not be demonstrative with your inner feelings and affections. All this adds up to a bit of a problem when you meet up with a Libra, whose ruling planet is Venus. We're talking harmony, love, artistic expression, and relationship orientation. He or she may feel stifled by your quiet reserve. Libra's artistic nature and flowing grace typically seeks a companion who is fair and just, and who can serve as a mirror to them in life. To your Libra mate, a life without sensitive sharing and beauty is flawed. The two of you are philosophically different and may have a difficult time finding the course of action that will suit each other's character. Yet if you have Venus in Aquarius or the Moon in any air sign, your compatibility is greatly increased. With shared values and mutual interests, you can be a welcome anchor for your flighty Libra. You can assist him or her in assembling a foundation of productivity and creative success, while your life is enriched by a new appreciation of the power of love, the enjoyment of the arts, and romantic partnership.

CAPRICORN IN LOVE

CAPRICORN & SCORPIO (OCT. 23–NOV. 21)

You naturally respect the personal privacy needs of those around you and tend to function best when secure boundaries are defined in your life. Scorpios can have the integrity and honesty you seek, even if they seem secretive at times. They'll tell the truth, but often not unless you ask. You can work and love well with a Scorpio, for they also keep their thoughts and feelings private, often preferring the quiet sanctuary of their own mind. Your Scorpio lover is intense and passionate, maybe more than you've bargained for, but he or she has a powerful sensuality that you find pleasing. Although you may not be inclined to display outward modes of affection, your sex drive can be quite strong and in Scorpio you have found someone who can go the distance with you. If however, your Venus is in physically detached Aquarius, problems may arise in this area. A water sign Moon in your birth chart will increase long-term compatibility. The two of you will work well together in any endeavor as both of you are highly focused when it comes to achieving your individual or mutual goals. You may create a trustworthy and passionate relationship that gives you each what you need, while at the same time creating a stable home.

CAPRICORN IN LOVE

CAPRICORN & SAGITTARIUS (NOV. 22–DEC. 21)

You're business oriented and know how to make the most out of any situation. You have an uncanny knowledge of what makes people tick. You may have an inner spirituality that can be overlooked by others. You're wise and enduring in work, and can be a rare friend once trust has been established. Although you are quite different in many ways, you can get along well with Sagittarius, primarily because you share an innate philosophy about life. The Archer's ruling planet is Jupiter, which symbolizes a prophetic type of person who shares ideas with an objective, open style. Capricorn is ruled by Saturn, which is more conservative, astute, and authoritative. You tend toward realism, even pessimism at times. The Archer is enthusiastic and inspirational, tending toward optimism, and sometimes denial of difficulty. You'll find your Sagittarius mate to be annoyingly restless as they seek adventure. He or she may find you restrictive as you hold back excitement or approval. If, however, you have the Moon or Mars in a fire sign, chances for compatibility is increased. In friendship and love, your Archer can brighten up your days and nights while you lend solid ground from which the two of you may thrive.

CAPRICORN IN LOVE

CAPRICORN & CAPRICORN (DEC. 22–JAN. 19)

When two of the same signs meet, there can be immediate chemistry and familiarity, for you both have similar natures. Yet each of you funnels the basic Capricorn qualities in a different manner. The undercurrents of your demeanor, however, are familiar, and therefore reassuring. You likely share an appreciation for each other's organizational capabilities, and you respect each other's responsible manner of living. You tend to be a controlling type, a take-charge kind of personality, clear about your boundaries of authority and power. Put two of you together in the same home or bed, and you're going to need to find a manageable balance of power. You may need to find ways to bring humor and play into your lives so as to elevate some of the burden you both carry. In this union, the placement of the Moon, Venus, and Mars can make or break compatibility. If you share air sign placements, you'll tend to be more light-hearted and talk about your situations as a way of dissipating the heaviness. If these planets are in fire signs, you'll probably move into action and work through your fears instead of talking about them. Together, you will create a stable home that is ordered and managed with discipline and love.

CAPRICORN IN LOVE

CAPRICORN & AQUARIUS (JAN. 20–FEB. 18)

Sometimes you need a nudge from an outside source to free you from some of the restraints of your personal expectations of yourself and others. When you hook up with a free-thinking Aquarius, who may be eccentric and independent in their style of living, you're in for a surprise. Your Aquarius lover can be rebellious and radical—and is not intimidated by the confines of rules and regulations. You, on the other hand, live within the bounds of the law and expect others to do the same. But Aquarius presents a convincing case for some rule-bending. They have an urge to pave a liberated path into the future, and you are intrigued by the prospects of joining them. It would help if the Moon in your chart is in an air sign, or better yet, if your Mercury or Venus is in Aquarius. No matter what, your view of the world is about to be changed. You may need to rearrange your old way of thinking and let go of certain concepts. On the other side of it, your lover must respect your boundaries and agree to adhere to some of your traditional values. Although your ways may never quite come together, you can be great friends or even lovers as you create a mature relationship based upon freedom and mutual respect.

CAPRICORN IN LOVE

CAPRICORN & PISCES (FEB. 19–MARCH 20)

Your responsible character gives others the message that you can carry the weight of the world on your shoulders, never needing help. You may be a mighty Goat, however, all too often you come to resent the role of authority and caretaker you've agreed to play in the lives of those you love. Avoid this scenario like the plague! Instead, try learning to flow with the rhythms of the people around you. Now, into your life comes a soft and compassionate Pisces partner, who melts your hard edges and invites you into their labyrinth of magic and enchantment. Do you have the courage to leave the real world behind? Is the spiritual and creative world of your Pisces love any less real than yours? You're captivated by the Fish's sheer elegance and magnetism. This union has great potential, especially if you can each get past your own self-limiting judgments. Compatibility is good to start, but gets even better if Venus in your chart is in Scorpio or Pisces, or if the Moon is in any water sign. Your Pisces lover will need to learn how to appreciate your order and focus—without judgment. If you can harmonize your authoritative personality with the dreamy, imaginative character of your Pisces mate, you can enjoy a lifetime of love and romance.

ABOUT THE AUTHORS

RICK LEVINE When I first encountered astrology as a psychology undergraduate in the late 1960s, I became fascinated with the varieties of human experience. Even now, I love the one-on-one work of seeing clients and looking at their lives through the cosmic lens. But I also love history and utilize astrology to better understand the longer-term cycles of cultural change. My recent DVD, *Quantum Astrology*, explores some of these transpersonal interests. As a scientist, I'm always looking for patterns in order to improve my ability to predict the outcome of any experiment; as an artist, I'm entranced by the mystery of what we do not and cannot know. As an astrologer, I am privileged to live in an enchanted world that links the rational and magical, physical and spiritual—and yes—even science and art.

JEFF JAWER I'm a Taurus with a Scorpio Moon and Aries rising who lives in the Pacific Northwest with Danick, my double-Pisces wife, our two very well-behaved teenage Leo daughters, and two black Gemini cats (who are not so well-behaved). I have been a professional astrologer since 1973. I encountered astrology as my first marriage was ending. I was searching and needed to understand myself better. Astrology filled the bill. More than thirty years later, it remains the creative passion of my life as I continue to counsel, write, study, and share ideas with clients and colleagues around the world.

ACKNOWLEDGMENTS

Thanks to Paul O'Brien, our agent, our friend, and the creative genius behind Tarot.com; Gail Goldberg, the editor who always makes us sound better; Charles Nurnberg and Michael Fragnito at Sterling Publishing, for their tireless support for the project; Barbara Berger, our supervising editor, who has shepherded this book with Taurean persistence and Aquarian invention; Laura Jorstad, for her refinement of the text; and Sterling project editor Mary Hern and designer Rachel Maloney for their invaluable help. We thank Bob Wietrak and Jules Herbert at Barnes & Noble, and all of the helping hands at Sterling. Thanks for the art and ideas from Jessica Abel and the rest of the Tarot.com team. Thanks as well to 3+Co. for the original design and to Tara Gimmer for the cover photo.

Tarot.com

A $5 GIFT CERTIFICATE
FOR YOUR CHOICE OF ASTROLOGY REPORTS OR TAROT READINGS!

Courtesy of Tarot.com for owners of
Your Personal Astrology Planner

Tarot.com is privileged to be the home of master astrologers Rick and Jeff... who are among the few living astrologers capable of writing an astrologically accurate book like this.

Because you have purchased *Your Personal Astrology Planner*, we want to honor you too... and invite you to experience your personal astrological makeup in much deeper detail. Visit us for reports written for your unique birth chart by Rick, Jeff, and other world class astrologers.

To redeem your Gift Certificate, go to

www.tarot.com/freegift2008

Your $5 Gift Certificate is simple to use, totally free, and there are no obligations

TAROT.COM   for Rick and Jeff's FREE horoscopes